REVIEW AND ASSESSMENT OF THE INDONESIA–MALAYSIA–THAILAND GROWTH TRIANGLE ECONOMIC CORRIDORS

THAILAND COUNTRY REPORT

Pawat Tangtrongjita

MARCH 2023

ASIAN DEVELOPMENT BANK

ADB

ISBN 978-92-9269-797-6 (print); 978-92-9269-798-3 (electronic); 978-92-9269-799-0 (ebook)
Publication Stock No. TCS220440-2
DOI: http://dx.doi.org/10.22617/TCS220440-2

Notes:
In this publication, "$" refers to United States dollars and "B" refers to Thai baht.

This publication is produced by ADB Technical Assistance (TA) 9572: Enhancing Effectiveness of Subregional Programs to Advance Regional Cooperation and Integration in Southeast Asia, which has funding support from the People's Republic of China Regional Cooperation and Poverty Reduction Fund, and the Republic of Korea e-Asia and Knowledge Partnership Fund.

Cover design by Mike Cortes.

CONTENTS

TABLES, FIGURES, AND MAPS

Tables

ACKNOWLEDGMENTS

This technical study was coordinated by a team in the Regional Cooperation and Operations Division (SERC), Southeast Asia Department of the Asian Development Bank (ADB). The technical study forms part of the analytical work produced under the ADB Technical Assistance 9572: Enhancing Effectiveness of Subregional Programs to Advance Regional Cooperation and Integration in Southeast Asia, which has funding support from the People's Republic of China Regional Cooperation and Poverty Reduction Fund, and the Republic of Korea e-Asia and Knowledge Partnership Fund.

The study was conducted by a team of consultants led by Carolina S. Guina, regional cooperation expert and team leader who provided specific guidance in carrying out the study and wrote the integrative report. A team of national consultants conducted the research on economic corridors in Indonesia, Malaysia, and Thailand and wrote the individual country reports. They are Sandy Nur Ikfal Raharjo (Indonesia), Abdul Rahim Anuar (Malaysia), and Pawat Tangtrongjita (Thailand).

Alfredo Perdiguero, director of SERC, and Gary Krishnan, senior country specialist supervised the study team. Maria Theresa Bugayong, senior operations officer (Resource Planning), and Jordana Queddeng-Cosme, consultant, provided technical and logistic support and coordinated the field visits where they also participated.

The Indonesia–Malaysia–Thailand Growth Triangle (IMT-GT) ministers Agus Suparmanto, minister of trade, Republic of Indonesia; Dato' Sri Mustapa Mohamed, minister in Prime Minister's Department (Economy), Malaysia; and Arkhom Termpittayapaisith, minister of finance, the Kingdom of Thailand, at the 26th IMT-GT Ministerial Meeting held in November 2020, provided overall strategic guidance in the course of reviewing the report.

The study benefited from the valuable inputs and insights of the senior officials, namely Rizal Affandi Lukman, and Raldi Hendro Koestoer, Coordinating Ministry for Economic Affairs of Indonesia; Saiful Anuar Bin Lebai Hussen, Noor Zari Bin Hamat, Mohd Shafiee B. Mohd Shah, and Sarimah Binti Amran, Economic Planning Unit, Prime Minister's Office of Malaysia; and Danucha Pitchayanan, Pattama Teanravisitsagool, and Wanchat Suwankitti, Office of the National Economic and Social Development Council of Thailand. The national secretariats worked closely with the team, especially the national consultants, in facilitating access to information and data, arranging and participating consultations with various stakeholders and meticulously reviewing the many drafts of the report. They are Netty Muharni, Tri Hidayatno, Sonny Ameriansah Soekoer of the Coordinating Ministry of Economic Affairs in Indonesia; Suhana Binti Md Saleh, Ahmad Zamri Bin Khairuddin, Balamurugan Ratha Krishnan, Nurul Ezzah Binti Md Zin, Mohammad Akhir Abdul Rahman, and Mattias Murphy Lai of the Economic Planning Unit, Prime Minister's Office in Malaysia; and Thuttai Keeratipongpaiboon, Chiraphat Chotipimai, Orachat Sungkhamanee, Potcharapol Prommatat, and Puntasith Charoenpanichpun of the Office of the National Economic and Social Development Council of Thailand. The Centre for IMT-GT Subregional Cooperation headed by Firdaus Dahlan and relevant IMT-GT working groups also provided insights.

The integrative report and country reports were copyedited by Maria Theresa Mercado and proofread by Maria Guia de Guzman and Jess Alfonso Macasaet. Michael Cortes handled typesetting, graphics generation, and designed the cover artwork. Pamela Asis-Layugan, Alona Mae Agustin, Raquel Tabanao, Nicole Marie Afable, Marianne Macabingkil, Cira Rudas, and Camille Genevieve Salvador provided overall assistance in the publications process. Angel Villarez and Rienzi Niccolo Velasco prepared the maps under the supervision of Abraham Villanueva and Carmela Fernando-Villamar. The ADB Department of Communications team provided invaluable assistance in design and publishing.

ABBREVIATIONS

ADB	Asian Development Bank
AH	Asian Highway
ASEAN	Association of Southeast Asian Nations
BCP	border crossing point
BIMSTEC	Bay of Bengal Initiative for Multi-Sectoral Technical and Economic Cooperation
BRI	Belt and Road Initiative
CAGR	compound annual growth rate
CDC	cargo distribution center
CIQ	customs, immigration, and quarantine
CMGF	Chief Ministers and Governors' Forum
CPO	crude palm oil
EC	economic corridor
ECRL	East Coast Rail Link
GDP	gross domestic product
GPP	gross provincial product
GRP	gross regional product
ICD	inland container depot
IMT-GT	Indonesia–Malaysia–Thailand Growth Triangle
JBC	Joint Business Council
JDS	Joint Development Strategy for Border Areas
km	kilometer
km^2	square kilometer
KTMB	Keretapi Tanah Melayu Berhad or Malayan Railways Limited
m^2	square meter
NESDC	National Economic and Social Development Council
PFAD	palm fatty acid distillate
PRC	People's Republic of China
RISDA	Rubber Industry Smallholders Development Authority
Ro-Ro	roll on, roll off
RPO	refined palm oil
RSS	ribbed smoked sheet
SBPAC	Southern Border Provinces Administrative Center
SEC	Southern Economic Corridor
SEZ	special economic zone
SMEs	small and medium-sized enterprises
SOM	Senior Officials Meeting
TEU	twenty-foot equivalent unit

CHAPTER

1

INTRODUCTION

Overview

On 1 October 2018 in Melaka, Malaysia, the 24th Indonesia–Malaysia–Thailand Growth Triangle (IMT-GT) Ministerial Meeting directed a review of existing IMT-GT economic corridors (ECs), and a study of the proposed sixth corridor linking Pattani–Yala–Narathiwat in Thailand with Perak and Kelantan in Malaysia, and with southern Sumatera in Indonesia. The countries requested technical assistance from the Asian Development Bank (ADB) in conducting this review.[1]

The economic corridor approach to development was first emphasized in the IMT-GT Road Map 2007–2011 as a key anchor for clustering major economic activities in the subregion. The IMT-GT Implementation Blueprint 2012–2016—the successor to the road map—included economic corridor development programs and projects among the flagship initiatives in the transport and energy sector. The importance of economic corridors was carried over to the Implementation Blueprint 2017–2021, which reaffirmed economic corridor development as a spatial framework to help achieve the IMT-GT 2036 Vision.

The IMT-GT strategic framework documents over the past years indicate the absence of a definitive framework for economic corridor development at a subregional level. The progress achieved so far is a result of independent national initiatives vetted through the IMT-GT platform, rather than from deliberate, evidence-based, corridor-wide subregional planning. This review is the first endeavor that looks at economic corridors from a wider perspective since it became a focus of IMT-GT economic cooperation in 2007.

Study Objectives

In assessing the IMT-GT economic corridors, this review aims to:
(i)   analyze the corridors' connections by road, rail, sea, and air;
(ii)   identify gaps in such connections, and recommend new routes for expansion of economic opportunities;
(iii) review the proposed sixth EC, and recommend its configuration;
(iv)   review links between ECs and the emerging subregional corridor network;
(v)   review ECs from a value chain perspective;
(vi)   recommend ways to improve EC development.

Methodology

As an initial activity, the study identified specific nodes in each corridor to establish the role of different economic units in relation to the major transport backbone and gateways. The nodes provided the reference points for assessing connectivity in the corridor. It also provided the basis for identifying linkages with potential nodes by expanding the corridor configuration based on emerging national strategies and economic opportunities. The nodes were classified according to the roles they perform: capital cities and urban areas, commercial nodes, border crossing points (BCPs), maritime gateway ports, tourism nodes, and interlink nodes.

---

[1]   C. S. Guina. 2023. *Review and Assessment of the Indonesia–Malaysia–Thailand Growth Triangle Economic Corridors: Integrative Report.* Manila: Asian Development Bank. The introduction was based on the integrative report, which is published as a separate publication.

The study considered possibilities for expanding existing corridors to other provinces and states. The motivation was to loop in strategically positioned areas in the government's spatial strategy into the regional economic corridors to derive additional benefits from continuity and scale effects. The expanded corridor would optimize regional spatial use by taking advantage of new production, growth and logistics centers located in a wider area, enhance supply chain opportunities, and contribute to a more equitable distribution of benefits. The additional provinces and states can upgrade to the main logistics routes that connect to other corridor networks, thus diversifying economic and social outcomes.

The study also looked at the value chain[2] of three major products in IMT-GT—palm oil, rubber, and halal foods—to get a broad perspective on the geography of their production, processing, and distribution components in the economic corridors. The geography of value chain components is the basis for determining the appropriate interventions to make the chain more efficient and their products, more competitive.

The study is qualitative and draws its observations and findings from inferences and interpretation of data collected from official and other sources. Desk research was conducted on IMT-GT documents, reports of meetings, references, and research materials. Fieldwork in Thailand was conducted with the team leader on 11–15 November 2019. The ministries and agencies involved in providing relevant information during the fieldwork are listed in Appendix 2.

The consultations covered many of the corridor provinces and involved meetings with the National Secretariat of Thailand, relevant line ministries, bodies responsible for spatial development programs or national corridors, provincial and state planning units, ports authorities, customs houses at BCPs, and the private sector (including representatives from the IMT-GT Joint Business Council [JBC]).

Several consultations with the national secretariat were also conducted in the course of the study. The representatives from various ministries and agencies that participated during the consultations with the national secretariat are also listed in Appendix 2.

Structure of the Report

The Thailand country report, which has been incorporated into the integrative report, is divided into eight chapters:

(i)   Introduction (Chapter 1),

(ii)   Development Context (Chapter 2),

(iii) Review of the Economic Corridors in Thailand (Chapter 3),

(iv) Proposed Route for Economic Corridor 6 (Chapter 4),

(v)   The Network of IMT-GT Economic Corridors (Chapter 5),

(vi) Economic Corridors from A Value Chain Perspective (Chapter 6),

(vii) Addressing Gaps in Institutional Mechanisms for Economic Corridor Development (Chapter 7), and

(viii) Summary of Findings and Recommendations (Chapter 8).

---

[2]   In this study, the distinction between the terms "value chain" and "supply chain" is not strictly applied. It is noted that a value chain is the process by which a company adds value to its raw materials to produce products eventually sold to consumers; while the supply chain represents all the steps required to get the product to the customer. Tarver, E. 2021. Value Chain vs. Supply Chain: *What's the Difference?* Investopedia. 2 August. https://www.investopedia.com/ask/answers/043015/what-difference-between-value-chain-and-supply-chain.asp#:~:text=The%20value%20chain%20is%20a,the%20product%20to%20the%20customer.

The study comes in four separate publications—the integrative report, which presents the overall findings from a subregional perspective, and individual county reports for Indonesia, Malaysia, and Thailand, which reflect the national perspectives.

Existing Economic Corridors

There are five existing IMT-GT economic corridors. The new economic corridor 6 (EC6) was proposed by Thailand at the 24th IMT-GT Ministerial Meeting in Melaka in October 2018. Thailand is involved in ECs 1, 2, and 5, and the proposed EC6. EC3 is a national corridor in Sumatera and EC4 covers only Indonesia and Malaysia. Map 1 presents the existing economic corridors.

The five existing economic corridors are as follows:

(i)   **Extended Songkhla–Penang–Medan Economic Corridor (EC1)**. EC1 consists of three main sections: two overland routes and a maritime route. The two overland routes connect (a) the Southern Thailand provinces of Nakhon Si Thammarat, Phatthalung, and Pattani with the international gateway in Songkhla, Yala, and Narathiwat; (b) an overland route from Songkhla to Penang; and (c) the maritime route that links Penang to Medan, the capital of North Sumatera, across the Strait of Malacca. Within North Sumatera, the important land connectivity is between Medan City and Belawan Port. Belawan Port in Medan is currently the main international port that supports this maritime connectivity segment. EC1 hosts some of the most agriculture-rich provinces in Southern Thailand that trade with Malaysia, Sumatera, and Singapore and play an important role in the supply chain of traded goods outside the subregion. EC1 covers several provinces in the border areas of Malaysia and Thailand and serves as the anchor for clustering major economic activities through the development of industrial hubs and special economic zones (SEZs).

(ii)   **Strait of Malacca Economic Corridor (EC2)**. EC2 is a coastal corridor connecting Thailand's southern provinces of Trang and Satun with Malaysia's states of Perlis, and on to Port Klang, Penang, and Melaka along the western coast. The maritime gateways in EC2 under the existing configuration are Tammalang Port (Satun), Port Klang (Selangor), Penang Port (Penang), and Tanjung Bruas Port (Melaka). The approach to corridor connectivity is multimodal, with land and coastal linkages. Due to the proximity of this corridor to Sumatera, there is considerable potential to complement the various stages of the production chain with the island, especially if a series of economic and industrial zones are established at strategic points along the corridor. This corridor has the potential to serve as a food hub, especially for halal, since food terminals and integrated food centers are being planned within the corridor.

(iii)   **Banda Aceh–Medan–Pekanbaru–Palembang Economic Corridor (EC3)**. EC3 is a national corridor in Sumatera. Connectivity among these provinces is envisaged to build traffic volume leading to Sumatera's international ports along its eastern coast—Banda Aceh, Medan, Pekanbaru, Dumai, and Jambi—are complementing coastal connectivity with ports in Penang and Melaka. This corridor, which is part of the Association of Southeast Asian Nations (ASEAN) Highway Network, is of critical importance for developing Sumatera, as well as an important building block for further enhancing connectivity within the IMT-GT subregion. Its development is closely linked with that of the other three corridors.

(iv)   **Melaka–Dumai Economic Corridor (EC4)**. EC4 is a maritime corridor linking Riau Province in Sumatera to the state of Melaka in Peninsular Malaysia. The underpinning economic rationale for this link is based on the strategic location of Dumai Port and Tanjung Bruas Port located opposite each other in one of the narrowest stretches of the Strait of Malacca, thus having the shortest distance between them across the Strait. The corridor includes the development of land connectivity to Dumai Port,

Map 1: Five Indonesia–Malaysia–Thailand Growth Triangle Economic Corridors

Source: Asian Development Bank.

as well as the development of Tanjung Bruas Port. EC4 has a long tradition of freight and passenger traffic between Sumatera and Malaysia. Dumai is the gateway port of Riau Province, one of the richest provinces of Indonesia with abundant palm oil plantations and onshore oil and gas resources. Dumai is principally a palm oil-related export port with general cargo, fertilizer, cement, and rice being the main import traffic.

(v)   **Ranong–Phuket–Aceh Economic Corridor (EC5)**. EC5 is mainly a maritime corridor linking ports in the northern part of Sumatera (mainly Ulee Lheue and Malahayati in Aceh Province) with Southern Thailand along its western coast facing the Andaman Sea, with the aim of exploiting tourism potentials. In Sumatera, Aceh Province is part of the corridor and Banda Aceh, the capital, and Sabang (located in the adjacent We Island) are the gateway and tourism nodes, respectively. EC5 is envisaged to enhance the connectivity between Sumatera and Southern Thailand primarily through the maritime mode. Connectivity was envisaged to be established through the development of facilities in key ports in Sumatera.

In Thailand, there are 14 provinces participating under the IMT-GT, nine of which are part of three existing IMT-GT economic corridors: ECs 1, 2, and 5. These nine provinces are Nakhon Si Thammarat, Songkhla, Narathiwat, Pattani, and Yala in EC1; Trang and Satun in EC2; and Ranong and Phuket in EC5. With the reconfiguration of these three existing corridors and the proposed route for EC6, the remaining five provinces have been included in economic corridors. All 14 provinces in Thailand have now been made part of the IMT-GT economic corridor network.

CHAPTER
2
DEVELOPMENT CONTEXT

Development Strategies for Southern Thailand

Thailand's regional cooperation initiatives for the IMT-GT cooperation focus on three interrelated factors: (i) the development of the country's southern provinces; (ii) the expansion of physical connectivity to trade gateways in the Strait of Malacca and farther to South Asia; and (iii) the development of value chains in rubber, palm oil, and halal foods.[3]

Thailand's Southern Development Plan and the Southern Economic Corridor (SEC) development plan have the main objectives of completing the overall picture of investment promotion. The southern development plan is the broad development framework therefore, the review of the southern development direction comprises the SEC development plan and related development guidelines that have specific targets and projects.

The main project of the SEC is a land bridge (road and rail) linking the coast of the Gulf of Thailand and the Andaman Sea coast. It aims to further exploit the potential of the agricultural product processing industry, develop the area toward world-class quality tourist destinations, and establish a complete transport and logistics network to accommodate the economic growth of the Bay of Bengal Initiative for Multi-Sectoral Technical and Economic Cooperation (BIMSTEC) and IMT-GT countries (Map 2).

The potential economic activities in the south consist of two main sectors: (i) agriculture focusing on rubber and palm oil as well as coastal fishery; and (ii) tourism, which has generated the highest revenue, second to Bangkok. Tourism is divided into the Andaman Sea and the Gulf of Thailand coasts, and southern border provinces. The southern provinces' border trade also constitutes the highest value in the country.

The conceptual framework of the SEC is based on existing geographic resources and economic activities, development of a new area for economic activities to generate new revenue sources, and distribution of development benefits from the former economic area. The development of the new economic area must focus on balanced management of natural resources and environment for long-term sustainability. The first phase will focus on two main sectors: (i) tourism; and (ii) bio-based industries consisting of food, bioenergy, and biomaterials.

The overall guidelines to develop the areas are as follows:

(i)   The development of trade gateways will consist of connecting networks and using them as routes to export goods on the west coast (via Ranong Port, Tammalang Pier, Wang Prachan Customs House in EC2 and EC5) to Thailand's Eastern Economic Corridor to BIMSTEC and IMT-GT countries.

(ii)   The development of tourism gateways in the Gulf of Thailand and the Andaman Sea has the objective of connecting the leading tourist destinations along the two seacoasts to become a new economic area in ecotourism. The development of the land bridge project connects Surat Thani–Nakhon Si Thammarat on the Gulf of Thailand with Phangnga–Phuket on the Andaman Sea. It involves the development of the transport route into a four-lane motorway, thus promoting economic, industrial, and tourism development in the areas traversed by the route. The route is divided into the route between Phuket–Surat Thani–Samui. Moreover, it is recommended to operate the extension between Phuket and Krabi. It will connect tourism along the two coasts. The Gulf of Thailand coast will focus on ecotourism in parallel with the preservation and conservation of the environment and natural resources, encouraging tourists to be acquainted with the old way of life of the local areas. The Andaman Sea coast will focus on marine tourism, health-related tourism, and cruise tourism.

---

[3]   ADB. 2021. *The Study on Thailand's Regional Cooperation and Integration Initiatives and Their Implication on Thailand's Development*. Consultant's report. Manila (TA-114852-THA).

(iii)   The development of bio-based and high-value agricultural processing industries that will turn the area into a center of agricultural processing and fishery. It is also the objective to enhance palm oil production in the area to generate high value-added goods by upgrading the capacity of local universities as centers of research and development for palm oil and rubber technologies and innovations. The areas including Surat Thani, Nakhon Si Thammarat, Songkhla, and Pattani are defined as pilot areas.

(iv)   The conservation of resources and culture for tourism will focus on the development of guidelines to conserve marine resources, forests, mangroves, and coral reefs to nurture the sources of marine life; the development of marine products; development of breeding and farming of lobsters, sea shrimps, and oysters; and conservation and dissemination of the local culture.

Development of Major Basic Infrastructure Projects in the Southern Economic Corridor

Transport and infrastructure development in the SEC aims to improve the domestic infrastructure and transport networks to link with neighboring countries, provide cross-border trade and investment facilitation, and make use of the border areas as gateways to international trade. Basic infrastructure projects include the construction of the new Sadao customs, immigration, and quarantine (CIQ) and upgrading of Padang Besar Customs house in Songkhla; expansion of Wang Prachan CIQ in Satun; upgrading of Betong Customs House in Yala; upgrading of Buketa Customs House and construction of the new Tak Bai CIQ in Narathiwat, construction of the second bridge in Narathiwat (near the new bridge over the Kolok River), construction of the bridge over the Kolok River in Tak Bai, Narathiwat–Tumpat, Kelantan; construction of the second bridge over the Kolok River in Su-ngai Kolok, Narathiwat–Rantau Panjang, Kelantan; as well as initiatives for the Green Cities in Songkhla (Hat Yai and Songkhla municipalities).

Trade and investment activities aim to develop potential border areas with neighboring countries. These would be supported by various development initiatives such as establishing Sadao–Kedah and Sadao–Perlis SEZs; and Narathiwat–Kelantan SEZ; the Thailand–Malaysia Rubber City Project; and IMT-GT Database of Trade, Investment, and Tourism.

Tourism development aims to realize the potential and joint development of the tourism industry with neighboring countries and development of historical and cultural tourist attractions to raise local pride and preserve national heritage.

Halal products and services cooperation will be strengthened to raise the quality of halal products and services in Songkhla and Pattani and neighboring countries to gain international recognition in the global market.

Human resource development will improve labor skills and uplift labor standards with neighboring countries to support skilled labor mobility and increase labor competitiveness in an expanded labor market in the IMT-GT.

The agriculture, agro-industry, and environment sectors will upgrade the agriculture sector to become part of a higher value-added production chain, raise income for farmers, promote advanced research and development to add value to products, and preserve the environment to assure sustainable development.

Socioeconomic Profile

Thailand's gross domestic product (GDP) in 2018 was valued at $338,345 million with the GDP per capita at $7,330. The average GDP growth rate during 2014–2018 was 3.55%. Thailand's economic structure relies mainly on services and manufacturing. The service sector accounts for 59.60% to total GDP. The most important contributors to the services sectors are tourism, retail sales, transportation, as well as banking and finance. Tourism is one of the biggest contributors to the sector. Industry accounts for 32.28% of Thailand's total production. The country's top manufacturing products include automobiles, hard disk drives, natural and synthetic rubber, textiles, etc. Most of the top manufacturing products are exported. Agriculture contributes to 8.12% to the total GDP. The socioeconomic profile of Thailand is on Table 1.

Table 1: Socioeconomic Profile of Thailand

Land Area	513,140 km²	Population	66.41 million (2018)
GDP ($ million in constant prices)			
2014	284,203.29	Urban population	22,873,538 (34.44%)
2018	338,345.08	Rural population	43,540,441 (65.56%)
Growth rate 2014–2018 (%)	3.55	**Population density**	
Share to GRP (%)		2005	121.64
Share to GDP (%)		2010	124.49
Rank in Thailand		2018	129.43
GDP per capita, 2018 ($)	7,330	**Labor and Employment**	
Agriculture Sector (%)	8.12	Economically active population	38,268,835
Service Sector (%)	59.60	Employed	37,864,550 (98.94%)
Industry Sector (%)	32.28	Unemployed	404,285 (1.06%)

GDP = gross domestic product, GRP = gross regional product, km² = square kilometer.
Source: Office of the National Economic and Social Development Board, 2019.

Map 2: Infrastructure in Southern Economic Corridor

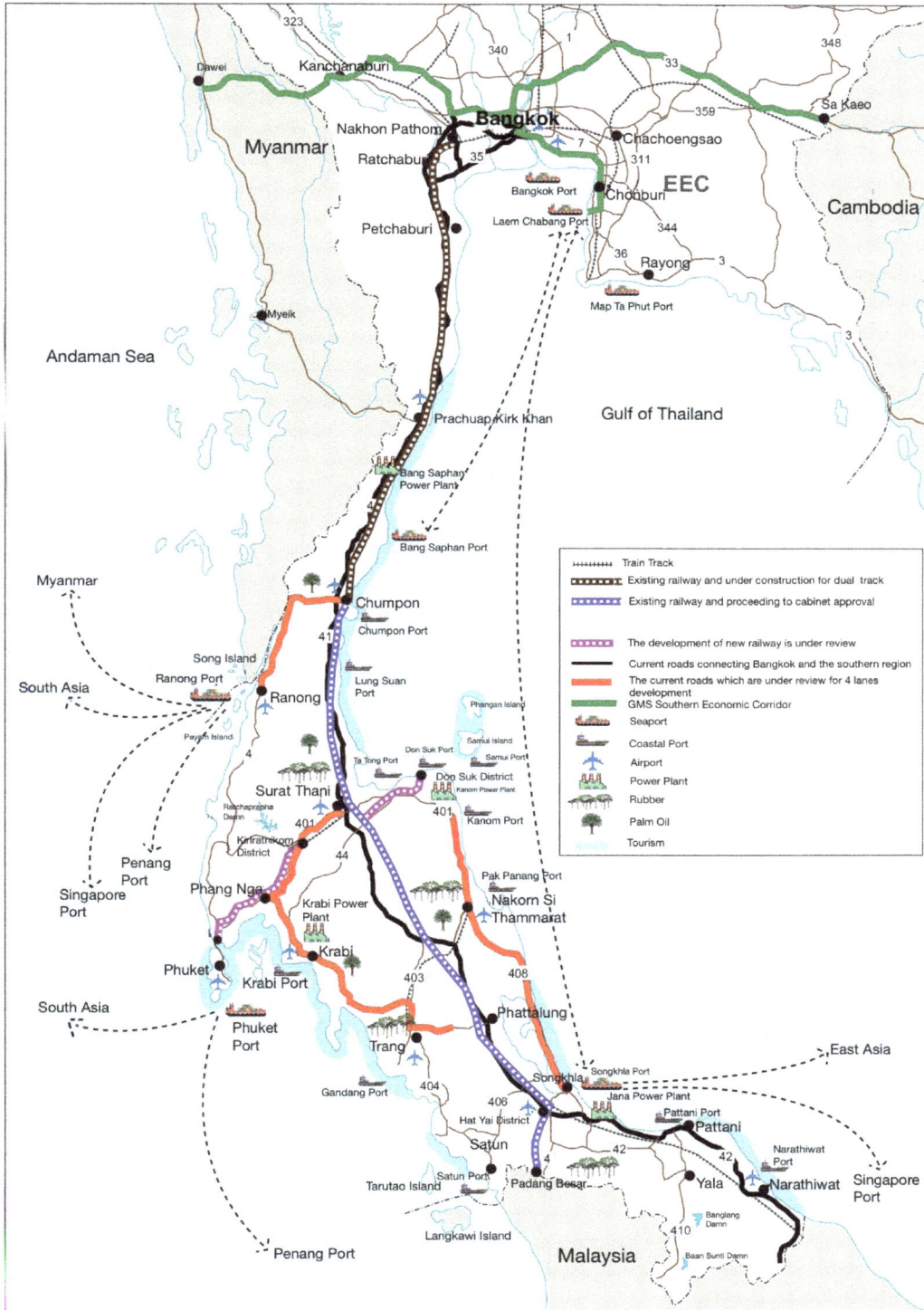

EEC = Eastern Economic Corridor.
Sources: Office of the National Economic and Social Development Council, (NESDC) 2019, https://www.nesdc.go.th/ewt_dl_link.php?nid=9557.

CHAPTER

3

REVIEW OF THE ECONOMIC CORRIDORS IN THAILAND

The three IMT-GT economic corridors in Thailand each have unique characteristics. Two corridors have overland links between economic centers in Malaysia and Thailand, complemented by maritime links to Sumatera ports in Medan (EC1), Strait of Malacca (EC2) and Aceh (EC5). The land and maritime links are supplemented by air services to facilitate the movement of high-value, less bulky cargo, as well as tourist passenger traffic, across the subregion.

Thailand's motivation for participating in the IMT-GT economic corridors are (i) the development of the southern provinces, (ii) the expansion of physical connectivity to trade gateways in the Strait of Malacca and farther to South Asia, and (iii) the development of the cross-border value chains.[4]

Economic Corridor 1. The Extended Songkhla–Penang–Medan Economic Corridor

Overview

The Extended Songkhla–Penang–Medan Economic Corridor (EC1) consists of three main sections: two overland routes and a maritime route. The two overland routes connect (i) the Southern Thailand provinces of Nakhon Si Thammarat, Phatthalung, and Pattani with the international gateway in Songkhla, Yala, and Narathiwat; (ii) an overland route from Songkhla to Penang; and (iii) the maritime route that links Penang to Medan, the capital of North Sumatera, across the Strait of Malacca (Map 3). Within North Sumatera, the important land connectivity is between Medan City and Belawan Port. Belawan Port in Medan is currently the main international port that supports this maritime connectivity segment.

At present, there are six provinces or states mentioned in EC1's descriptive name (Nakhon Si Thammarat, Songkhla, Kedah, Perlis, Penang, and North Sumatera). Originally, the route for EC1 covered these three other provinces in Thailand: Songkhla and extended southward to Pattani, Yala, and Narathiwat. These three provinces in the southernmost branch are now proposed to form part of the new EC6 connecting Kelantan. The analysis of these three provinces therefore will be covered in the discussion of EC6 in Chapter 4.

---

[4]   ADB. 2021. *The Study on Thailand's Regional Cooperation and Integration Initiatives and Their Implication on Thailand's Development*. Consultant's report. Manila (TA-114852-THA). p.43.

Map 3: Extended Songkhla–Penang–Medan Economic Corridor
(Economic Corridor 1)

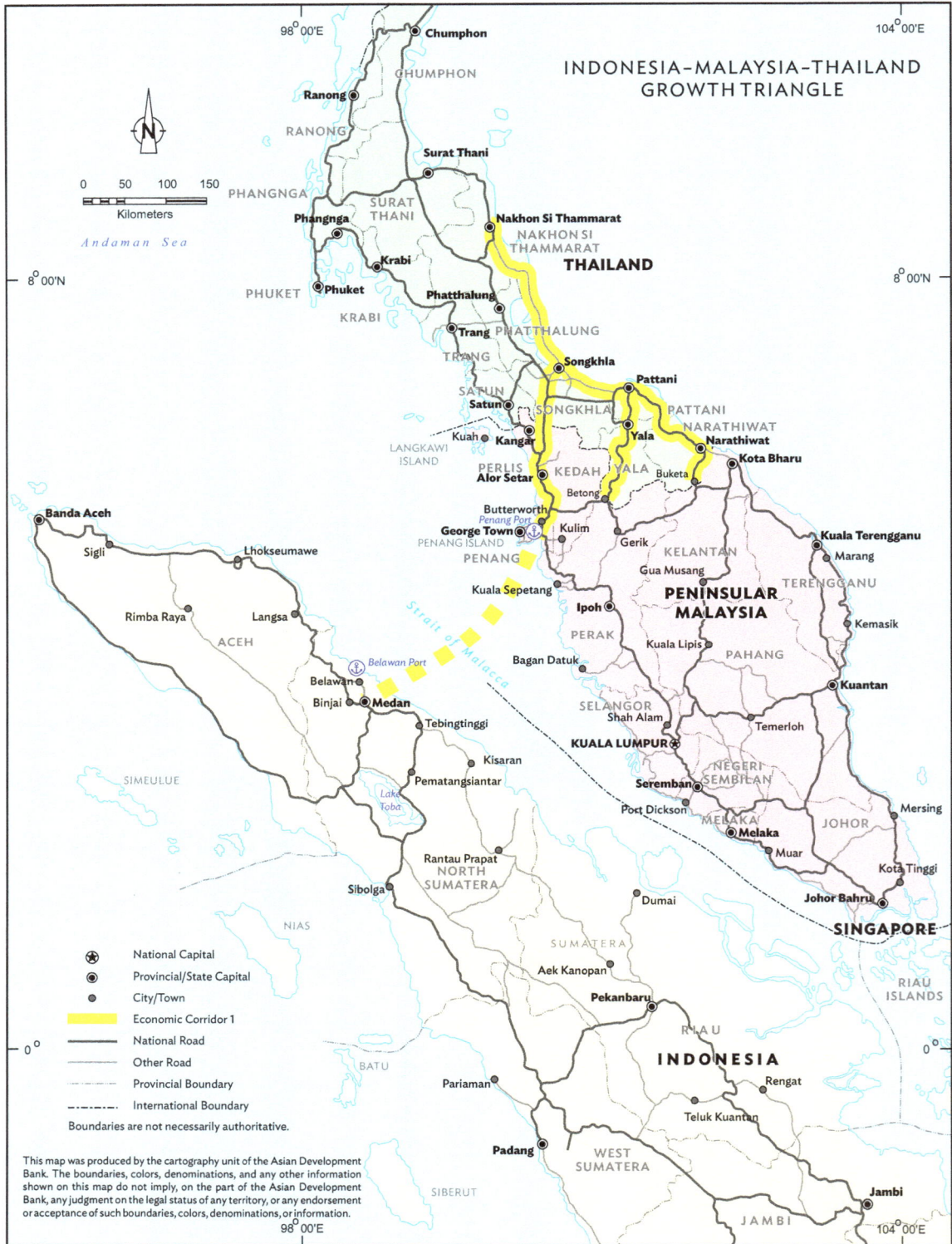

INDONESIA–MALAYSIA–THAILAND
GROWTH TRIANGLE

Source: Asian Development Bank.

Existing Provinces and Nodes

Nakhon Si Thammarat. Nakhon Si Thammarat, a large province in Southern Thailand in terms of population, is well-known for the ancient city of world heritage and Srivichai historical sites. Nakhon Si Thammarat is a province connecting Surat Thani and Songkhla, which will support EC1 as a tourist destination and a center for natural rubber production for processing along the corridor.

Nakhon Si Thammarat's 2018 gross provincial product (GPP) was $3,054 million with the GPP per capita at $3,375. The provincial production structure ratio comprises the service sector (49.8%), the agriculture sector (26.2%), and the industry sector (23.9%) (Table 2).

Table 2: Socioeconomic Profile of Nakhon Si Thammarat Province

Land Area	9,943 km²	Population of Thailand	66.41 million (2018)
GPP ($ million in constant prices)		Of which, in Nakhon Si Thammarat	1,560,433 (2.3%)
2014	2,793.2	Urban population	297,515 (19.0%)
2018	3,054.4	Rural population	1,262,918 (80.9%)
Growth rate 2014–2018 (%)	2.2	**Population density**	
Share to GRP (%)	11.5	2005	151.3
Share to GDP (%)	0.92	2010	153.1
Rank in Southern Region	4	2018	156.9
GPP per capita, 2018 ($)	3,375	**Labor and Employment**	
Agriculture Sector (%)	26.2	Economically active population	899,576
Service Sector (%)	49.8	Employed	888,709 (98.7%)
Industry Sector (%)	23.9	Unemployed	10,867 (1.2%)

GDP = gross domestic product, GPP = gross provincial product, GRP = gross regional product, km² = square kilometer.
Source: Office of the National Economic and Social Development Board, 2019.

Songkhla. Songkhla serves as a southern industrial hub and a collection area for agricultural products coming from within the province and adjacent provinces for processing and distribution to domestic consumers as well as exports via the Thai–Malaysian border. Most agro-processing industries (e.g., seafood, rubber, rubber wood) are in Songkhla district, in the vicinity of the Songkhla Industrial Estate and Songkhla Port (Table 3).

Songkhla had a large population of 1.4 million or 2.1% of Thailand's population in 2018. Its GPP per capita of $4,701 is the highest in the southern region. Songkhla's 2018 GPP, valued at $5,119 million, comprises 20% of GRP. The province hosts most commercial and industrial activities in the south. The provincial production structure ratio comprises the service sector (54.9%), the agriculture sector (12.4%) and the industry sector (32.6%).

Hat Yai. Hat Yai is the largest city of Songkhla Province, the largest metropolitan and commercial area in the south, and the third-largest metropolitan area of the country. It is about 36 kilometers (km) to Songkhla Port, which has a capacity of 2.1 million tons of cargo a year, and transports goods between the south and the central plains of Thailand. Songkhla Port also serves as an important maritime gateway for transporting goods to the Thai–Malaysian border headed to Penang Port in Malaysia, and connects with Map Ta Phut in Rayong Province, which is part of the Greater Mekong Subregion (GMS).

Table 3: Socioeconomic Profile of Songkhla Province

Land Area	7,394 km²	Population of Thailand	66.41 million (2018)
GPP ($ million in constant prices)		Of which, in Songkhla	1,432,628 (2.1%)
2014	4,769.0	Urban population	729,928 (50.9%)
2018	5,119.1	Rural population	702,700 (49.0%)
Growth rate 2014–2018 (%)	1.7	Population density	
Share to GRP (%)	19.3	2005	176.1
Share to GDP (%)	1.5	2010	183.5
Rank in Southern Region	1	2018	193.7
GPP per capita, 2018 ($)	4,701	Labor and Employment	
Agriculture Sector (%)	12.4	Economically active population	888,759
Service Sector (%)	54.9	Employed	863,535 (97.1%)
Industry Sector (%)	32.6	Unemployed	25,224 (2.8%)

GDP = gross domestic product, GPP = gross provincial product, GRP=gross regional product, km² = square kilometer.
Source: Office of the National Economic and Social Development Board, 2019.

Socioeconomic Profile of the Southernmost Provinces

Pattani, Yala, and Narathiwat are the southernmost provinces in Southern Thailand located in the eastern part bordering Kedah, Perak, and Kelantan in Malaysia. The three provinces are among the economically lagging provinces in the southern region. During 2014–2018, Pattani's GPP registered a negative growth rate of 2.47% while Yala's grew at 1.4%, and Narathiwat's GPP grew at 2.5%—placing the three provinces at the lower rung of Southern Thailand's economy. GPP per capita in Yala is $2,841; in Pattani, $2,342; and in Narathiwat, $1,920. Around 70%–80% of the population in the three provinces live in the rural areas. About one-third of the economy is based on agriculture and around 60% on the service sector.

Pattani's economy relies mainly on the agriculture sector, especially fishery and fishery-related industries (Table 4). Tourism is Pattani's second source of revenue with several historical and archaeological sites that connect to the history of Malaysia. Pattani also has a policy to promote the halal food industry, especially at households and small and medium-sized enterprises (SMEs).

Table 4: Socioeconomic Profile of Pattani Province

Land Area	1,940 km²	Population of Thailand	66.41 million (2018)
GPP ($ million in constant prices)		Of which, in Pattani	718,077 (1.08%)
2014	1,112.91	Urban population	128,380 (17.88%)
2018	1,006.90	Rural population	589,697 (82.12%)
Growth rate 2014–2018 (%)	–2.47	Population density	
Share to GRP (%)	3.80	2005	327.00
Share to GDP (%)	0.30	2010	337.76
Rank in Southern Region	9	2018	370.14
GPP per capita, 2018 ($)	2,342	Labor and Employment	
Agriculture Sector (%)	24.80	Economically active population	315,926
Service Sector (%)	63.86	Employed	303,953 (96.21%)
Industry Sector (%)	11.34	Unemployed	11,972 (3.79%)

– = negative, GDP = gross domestic product, GPP = gross provincial product, GRP = gross regional product, km² = square kilometer.
Source: Office of the National Economic and Social Development Board, 2019.

Yala has over 200,000 hectares of rubber plantations that produce rubber latex and rubber wood that are supplied as raw materials for processing in the city or nearby provinces. The intermediate or finished products are exported through Betong BCP, which is well-positioned for nearby Malaysian markets or exports to Penang and other areas. Tourism is important to Betong because of the large number of Malaysians crossing the border to visit tourist destinations in Thailand. Betong and Su-ngai Kolok export rubber latex and fruits to Malaysia through Betong border crossing whereas Su-ngai Kolok imports lumber and exports rubber from Malaysia. Table 5 shows the socioeconomic profile of Yala Province.

Table 5: Socioeconomic Profile of Yala Province

Land Area	4,521 km^2	**Population of Thailand**	66.41 million (2018)
GPP ($ million in constant prices)		Of which, in Yala	532,326 (0.80%)
2014	697.75	Urban population	143,420 (26.94%)
2018	738.67	Rural population	388,906 (73.06%)
Growth rate 2014–2018 (%)	1.43	**Population density**	
Share to GRP (%)	2.79	2005	102.66
Share to GDP (%)	0.22	2010	107.80
Rank in Southern Region	10	2018	117.75
GPP per capita, 2018 ($)	2,841	**Labor and Employment**	
Agriculture Sector (%)	31.17	Economically active population	224,130
Service Sector (%)	58.92	Employed	221,197 (98.69%)
Industry Sector (%)	9.91	Unemployed	(1.31%)

GDP = gross domestic product, GPP = gross provincial product, GRP = gross regional product, km^2 = square kilometer.
Source: Office of the National Economic and Social Development Board, 2019.

Narathiwat's development policies focus on halal, rubber, and rubber wood industries linked to Special Border Economic Zone cluster development in Nong Chik, Narathiwat. The use of border networks in Buketa, Su-ngai Kolok, and Tak Bai will increase cross-border investment, trade, and tourism. The socioeconomic profile of Narathiwat Province is in Table 6.

Three pilot development districts—Betong, Nong Chik, and Su-ngai Kolok—have been designated as special economic areas where investments can enjoy additional tariff and nontariff incentives over and above those offered in other areas. The construction of new bridge and CIQ facilities in border towns can expand cross-border trade in fruits and vegetables from Thailand, as well as collaboration with Malaysia in halal, furniture, and other industrial clusters.

Map 4: Extended Songkhla–Penang–Medan Economic Corridor
(Economic Corridor 1) - Thailand

Source: Asian Development Bank.

Table 6: Socioeconomic Profile of Narathiwat Province

Land Area	4,475 km²	Population of Thailand	66.41 million (2018)
GPP ($ million in constant prices)		Of which, in Narathiwat	802,474 (1.21%)
2014	656.65	Urban population	170,804 (21.28%)
2018	724.50	Rural population	631,670 (78.72%)
Growth rate 2014-2018 (%)	2.49	**Population density**	
Share to GRP (%)	2.73	2005	156.54
Share to GDP (%)	0.22	2010	164.73
Rank in Southern Region	11	2018	179.32
GPP per capita, 2018 ($)	1,920	**Labor and Employment**	
Agriculture Sector (%)	31.02	Economically active population	345,267
Service Sector (%)	61.14	Employed	321,133 (93.01%)
Industry Sector (%)	7.84	Unemployed	(6.99%)

GDP = gross domestic product, GPP = gross provincial product, GRP = gross regional product, km² = square kilometer.
Source: Office of the National Economic and Social Development Board, 2019.

Status of Physical Connectivity

Road Connectivity

The Extended Songkhla–Penang–Medan Economic Corridor (EC1) in Thailand starts in Surat Thani and ends at the Thai–Malaysian BCP (Map 4). It is divided into nine sections: (i) Nakhon Si Thammarat Mueang District–Phatthalung Mueang District, (ii) Phatthalung Mueang District–Hat Yai District, (iii) Songkhla Mueang District–Hat Yai District, (iv) Songkhla-Padang Besar BCP, (v) Songkhla–Sadao BCP, (vi) Songkhla–Ban Prakop BCP, (vii) Hat Yai–Padang Besar BCP, (viii) Hat Yai-Sadao BCP, and (ix) Hat Yai–Ban Prakop BCP. The details of the current physical status and conditions of each route are in Table 7. Overall, road connectivity in EC1 covers the distance between 30.6 km and 140 km depending on the start and end points (Table 7). All routes are safe, equipped with traffic signs, traffic lines, and complete and undamaged safety equipment, curved guideposts, and complete guardrail in good condition. The road surface is smooth in the entire route.

Table 7: Economic Corridor 1: Start and End Points in Thailand

Start Point	End Point	Route	Distance (km)	Traffic Lanes	Road Classification	Road Condition
Nakhon Si Thammarat	Phatthalung	403/AH2	110	4	Class I	Good
Phatthalung	Hat Yai	4	98	4	Class I	Good
Songkhla	Hat Yai	414/407	30.6	4	Class I	Good
Songkhla	Padang Besar	407/414/413/4/4054	90	4	Class I	Good
Songkhla	Sadao	407/414/4135/4/4054	90	4	Class I	Good
Songkhla	Ban Prakop	407/4	84.9	4/2	Class I	Good
Hat Yai	Padang Besar	4135/4/4054	54.4	4	Class I	Good
Hat Yai	Sadao	4	56.7	4	Class I	Good
Hat Yai	Ban Prakop	4/42/408	86.9	4/2	Class I	Good

AH = Asian Highway.
Source: Compiled by the author.

Rail Connectivity

The Southern Line splits at Hat Yai into two routes. The main route goes southeast to Su-ngai Kolok on the Thai–Malaysian border. The other routes go southwest to Padang Besar and other destinations in Malaysia to Kantang Port (Trang) at the Andaman Sea. The rail route from Hat Yai and Padang Besar BCP covers a distance of 45 km.

Cross-Border Nodes

Cross-border nodes in EC1 consist of three BCPs in Padang Besar, Sadao, and Ban Prakop (Table 8). Overall, the distance between cross-border nodes ranges from 25.1 km to 70.3 km. All roads are well equipped and are in good condition.

Table 8: Distance between Cross-Border Nodes

Start Point	End Point	Route	Distance (km)	Traffic Lanes	Road Classification	Road Condition
Ban Prakop BCP	Sadao BCP	408/4243/4	68.1	4	Class I	Good
Sadao BCP	Padang Besar BCP	4/4054	25.1	4	Class I	Good
Ban Prakop BCP	Padang Besar BCP	408/4243	70.3	4	Class I	Good

BCP = border crossing point, km = kilometer.
Notes: Route between both BCPs is mostly on Highway 4243, which has two traffic lanes and cannot be extended as it passes through the preserved forests in a mountainous region. There is very little transport on the route.
Source: Compiled by the author.

The standards of customs services of the three customs houses were referenced to the standards of Thailand's customs services and have a duration of about 5–34 minutes, depending on the procedures. The details are in Table 9.

Table 9: Standards of Thailand's Customs Services for Import–Export Procedures

Procedures	Estimated Time Duration	Customs Standards
1 Transmission of entrepreneur information via electronic system	Within 5 minutes	From the time bill of lading enters the department's electronics system until it comes out with the number of the bill of lading.
2 Inspection of goods with x-ray machine	Within 15 minutes	From the time container or vehicle passes the x-ray machine until the officer finishes processing and analyzing the information.
3 Opening of goods for inspection	Within 30 minutes	From the time the entrepreneur or representative submits documents to the officer for inspection of goods until the officer releases the goods (excluding the time for preparation of goods and in case the officer has doubt or finds irregularity requiring detailed inspection).
4 Payment of duty or guarantee with cash or guarantee document	Within 6 minutes	From start to finish the time the entrepreneur or representative submits documents to the officer to pay duty or place guarantee.
5 Inspection of accompanying belongings of transit passengers in Thailand via airplane in red lane	Within 25 minutes	Starts from the time passenger contacts officer at the red lane until officer inspects and notifies of duty (if applicable).
6 Random inspection of passenger's luggage and accompanying belongings with x-ray machine (if there is no suspect case) in case of transit in Thailand via airplane	Within 5 minutes/ luggage	Starts from luggage and accompanying belongings inspected by x-ray machine and the officer finishes information processing and analysis if there is no suspect case.
7 Release of goods via post (in case it does not require bill of lading and consideration from other agencies)	Within 34 minutes	From start to finish when the service recipient submits request form to receive goods and receive the goods released from Customs Department.

Source: Customs Department, Ministry of Finance. 2012. Thai Customs Service Standards. https://www.customs.go.th/data_files/0181ca375e441366e6e4e75 aae06a05e.pdf (accessed 26 February 2020).

Maritime Connectivity

Songkhla Port. Songkhla Port is the main port in EC1. The port was constructed in 1986 and Chao Phraya International Port Company Limited, a private company, has been operating the port since 1988.[5] The length of the pier is 501 meters, and the depth is 120 meters. The container yard is 50,000 square meters (m^2) and the warehouse facilities cover 6,700 m^2. Overall, the entire pier covers 115,200 m^2. The port capacity is 2.1 million tons of cargo a year. For containers, the capacity is 200,000 twenty-foot equivalent units (TEU) a year. In the past 6 years, the number of ships entering the port each year varied from 338 to 550. About half are container ships.

The port's outbound cargo by value is composed of (i) wood and wood products (52%), (ii) canned foods (17%), (iii) rubber (13%), (iv) latex gloves (7%), (v) frozen fish and other products (7%), (vi) construction materials (1%), and (vii) other products (3%). Inbound cargo by value consists of (i) frozen foods (44%), (ii) chemical products (18%), (iii) machinery (11%), (iv) animal feeds (7%), (v) construction materials (3%), and (vi) others (17%).

---

[5]   According to the Department of Marine, the Treasury Department is in the process of selecting a new port operator. It requested the Office of the Attorney General to consider the draft joint venture contract. The Office of the Attorney General's recommendation will be considered by the Cabinet. The contract is expected to be signed by 2022.

There are three major limitations to the existing port. First, the maximum draft for a ship is 8 meters, and a large ship cannot exceed a draft of 7.7 meters. The size of a ship is limited to a maximum overall length of 173 meters, and a beam not to exceed 25 meters. Second, the size of the container yard is already near full capacity. With the load-bearing limit of the pier, intermodal container guidelines indicate a maximum stacking of three containers. However, they are currently being densely positioned at six stacks based on a "last-in, first-out" strategy. Third, there are no front cranes for loading and unloading containers and other cargo. All ships must have their own built-in cranes.

Songkhla's maximum draft for ships is much less than Penang Port's draft limitation of 11 meters for ships. As regards container storage, the main logistics operations at container terminals include berth allocation, stowage planning, crane scheduling, terminal transport optimization, and storage and stacking logistics. Container stacking policy affects the productivity of the port and retrieval time. Commercial inventory of containers is almost evenly divided between 20-foot and 40-foot containers. This means that about two-thirds of all containerized cargo is shipped in 40-foot containers because they have twice the capacity.

In comparison, Penang Port has a much larger container yard that enables it to handle more cargo and has dedicated shipping service to Japan and the People's Republic of China (PRC), without having to go to another port. It also has many empty containers arriving from the Middle East, with the result that containers are readily available for export of goods. Additionally, Penang Port has 13 quay gantry cranes (QGCs). Out of these seven are post Panamax QGCs capable of handling vessels with one row of containers across with a declared productivity rate of 25 moves per hour per crane. Berth capacity currently is at 2 million TEUs per annum.

While space is limited, improvements in the distribution of facilities are being planned to create more efficiency and reduce operating costs. The improvements include (i) re-arranging the port layout, (ii) improving the front posture to place the 350 meters rail and install three cranes, and (iii) moving and improving the port entrance. The resulting rearrangements will increase capacity to about 500,000 TEUs a year, compared with the existing 200,000 TEUs yearly capacity. However, the government has yet to approve these planned improvements. At present, there is a need for a clear and consistent government policy on the development of Songkhla Port to avoid or minimize uncertainties. For instance, Songkhla Port Administration is granted only short-term concessions, thus preventing it from investing in up-to-date equipment to improve port efficiency.

Songkhla 2 Port Project. The Songkhla 2 Port Project of the Harbor Department is proposed to be in the Na Tab Subdistrict, Chana District, Songkhla Province—about 40 km south of the existing Songkhla Port. The proposed size is 900 meters wide and 1,200 meters long. Songkhla Port 2 is being planned to connect to Penang Port through a land bridge that will reduce the time of transporting goods between two ocean ports.

The Harbor Department has conducted the detailed study, survey, and design, as well as public hearings for the proposed project. The project is currently at the environmental health impact assessment stage. The Harbor Department has conducted a study for developing the area behind Songkhla Port 2 into a logistics center and the Chana Industrial Estate. The Harbor Department and the Port Authority of Thailand have also developed a plan for marine transport services to be provided from Laem Chabang and Sriracha Port to Songkhla Port to reduce congestion in transporting goods from southern Thailand to Bangkok Metropolitan Region. The route is also an alternative for transporting and distributing goods from Southern Thailand to other regions in the country and to the GMS countries.

Air Linkages

The airport in EC1 is the Hat Yai International Airport. It is operated by the Airports of Thailand Public Company Limited. Hat Yai International Airport is an important airport because it is the gateway for Muslims' pilgrimage to Mecca, Saudi Arabia. Hat Yai International Airport is ranked fifth among the country's airports following Suvarnabhumi Airport, Don Mueang International Airport, Phuket Airport, and Chiang Mai Airport, respectively. As of 2018, the airport received 4.9 million passengers, 9,203 flights, and 12,965 tons of goods. At present, Hat Yai International Airport is revising its master plan and airport traffic demand forecast.

There is no direct flight from Hat Yai International Airport to provinces and states in EC1. The only flight to Malaysia is to Kuala Lumpur. The six airlines currently operating at the airport are flying domestic routes, while three airlines operate international routes to Medina and Jeddah (chartered flights for the Hajj), Kuala Lumpur, and Singapore (Table 10).

Table 10: Flight Routes from Hat Yai International Airport

Airlines	Destinations	Types of Flights
Thai Smile Airways	Bangkok–Suvarnabhumi	Domestic
	Bangkok–Don Mueang	Domestic
Thai AirAsia	Bangkok–Don Mueang, Chiang Mai, U Tapao, Khon Kaen	Domestic
Thai Lion Air	Bangkok–Don Mueang, Udon Thani	Domestic
Bangkok Airways	Phuket	Domestic
New Gen Airways	Bangkok–Don Mueang, Phitsanulok, Chiang Mai, Khon Kaen, Narathiwat (chartered flights)	Domestic
Saudi Arabian Airlines	Medina (outgoing), Jeddah (incoming) (chartered flights for the Hajj)	International
Thai AirAsia	Kuala Lumpur	International
Scoot	Singapore	International

Source: Compiled by the author.

The route to Hat Yai International Airport from the city center uses Highway 4135 with four traffic lanes. The road surface is smooth in the entire section. The route is safe, equipped with traffic signs, traffic lines, complete and undamaged safety equipment, curved guideposts, and complete guardrail in good condition. Public transportation is available to Hat Yai International Airport.

Trade

In 2018, the trade flows at the Thai–Malaysian border in Songkhla was valued at $17,605 million representing a compounded average increase of about 2.9% from 2014 (Table 11). Exports increased by 1.6%, while imports rose even faster by 4.5% (Table 12). Thailand enjoyed a surplus of $438.4 million.

Table 11: Export–Import Value at Thai–Malaysian Border in Songkhla

Province	Trade Value ($ million)					CAGR (%)
	2014	2015	2016	2017	2018	
Songkhla	15,657.9	14,996.6	15,329.2	17,317.2	17,604.9	2.9
Export	8,463.0	7,707.9	7,929.4	9,575.5	9,021.7	1.6
Import	7,194.9	7,288.7	7,462.8	7,741.7	8,583.2	4.5

CAGR = compound annual growth rate.
Sources: Department of Foreign Trade, 2019; Bank of Thailand. https://www.bot.or.th/App/BTWS_STAT/statistics/ReportPage.aspx?reportID=123&language=th (accessed 26 February 2020).

Table 12: Export–Import Value at Customs Houses in Songkhla

Customs Houses	Trade Value ($ million)					CAGR (%)
	2014	2015	2016	2017	2018	
Sadao Customs House	**10,895.7**	**10,150,890**	**10,396,270**	**10,897,220**	**11,774,060**	**1.9**
Export	4,875.4	4,482,110	4,602,030	5,173,430	5,383,170	2.5
Import	6,020.3	5,668,780	5,794,240	5,723,790	6,390,890	1.5
Padang Besar Customs House	**4,746.4**	**4,830,230**	**4,968,300**	**6,373,520**	**5,777,830**	**5.0**
Export	3,571.7	3,210,320	3,301,750	4,368,820	3,588,480	0.12
Import	1,174.7	1,619,910	1,666,550	2,004,700	2,189,350	16.8
Ban Prakop Customs House	**15.9**	**15,490**	**27,710**	**46,520**	**52,990**	**35.1**
Export	15.8	15.4	25.7	33.3	50.0	33.2
Import	0.60	0.1	2.0	13.3	2.9	739.4
Total	**15,658.0**	**14,996.6**	**15,392.2**	**17,317.2**	**17,604.8**	**2.9**

CAGR = compound annual growth rate.
Sources: Department of Foreign Trade, 2019; Bank of Thailand. https://www.bot.or.th/App/BTWS_STAT/statistics/ReportPage.aspx?reportID=123&language=th (accessed 26 February 2020).

In 2018, the major export and import products via Sadao Customs House were automatic data processing machines, machine parts and components, linear or rotary internal combustion engines, integrated circuit and micro-assembly used in electronics and electric motors and generators (excluding generator set) (Table 13). The similar export and import products indicate that Thailand and Malaysia share the electronic appliances and auto parts supply chain between them (Table 14).

Table 13: Sadao Customs House: Top 10 Export–Import Values in 2018

Rank	Export	Weight (kg)	Value ($ million)	Import	Weight (kg)	Value ($ million)
1	Natural rubber	688,837,710	762.9	Automatic data processing machines	6,792,513	1,220,919
2	Automatic data processing machines	3,987,537	647.6	Disks, tapes, and storage devices	5,503,813	647,830
3	Machine parts and components	3,485,520	530.2	Machine parts and components	18,849,092	530,587
4	Linear or rotary internal combustion engines	194,501	500.9	Linear or rotary internal combustion engines	246,284	523,687
5	Processed para wood	694,241,401	278.1	Integrated circuit and micro-assembly used in electronics	741,506	521.4
6	Integrated circuit and micro-assembly used in electronics	493,173	165.8	Accumulators	2,654,328	142.9
7	Rubber gloves	31,354,610	153.5	Diode, transistors, and other similar semiconductors	1,487,553	139.0
8	Electric motors and generators (excluding generator set)	5,417,281	130.9	Other items made of iron or steel	22,316,291	135.4
9	Particle boards and other similar boards	495,811,579	101.2	Keyboards, consoles, panels, tables, cabinets, and other supports to control or distribute electricity	1,196,204	79.8
10	Automotive parts and components	9,827,395	95.8	Other items made of aluminum	2,154,341	78.9

kg = kilogram.
Sources: Sadao Customs House, 2019; Bank of Thailand. https://www.bot.or.th/App/BTWS_STAT/statistics/ReportPage.aspx?reportID=123&language=th (accessed 26 February 2020).

Table 14: Padang Besar Customs House: Top 10 Export–Import Values in 2018

Rank	Export	Weight (kg)	Value ($ million)	Import	Weight (kg)	Value ($ million)
1	Natural rubber	1,188,297,229	1,616.2	Recording media	8,553,136	1,067.3
2	Synthetic rubber	506,737,917	769.6	Televisions	2,686,586	80.5
3	Sawn wood	528,213,076	207.8	Automotives and other vehicles designed mainly for passenger transport	2,569,674	61.5
4	Automotive parts and components	26,425,539	166.6	Machine parts and components	1,115,617	56.8
5	Automatic data processing machines	774,180	62.8	Printing press	2,052,138	48.9
6	Electric cutting tools	3,199,331	60.9	Automatic data processing machines	386,708	46.1
7	Fiberboard made from wood	149,533,396	40.9	Electric cutting tools	1,107,791	45.7
8	Malt extract	6,419,867	39.8	Automotive parts and components	2,180,129	33.5
9	Parts for specific use	1,987,940	26.9	Unwrought tin	1,397,000	28.8
10	Recording media	229,792	25.5	Other items made of iron or steel	6,883,568	26.9

kg = kilogram.
Sources: Padang Besar Customs House, 2019; Bank of Thailand. https://www.bot.or.th/App/BTWS_STAT/statistics/ReportPage.aspx?reportID=123&language=th (accessed 26 February 2020).

In 2018, the value of exports via Ban Prakop Customs House with the highest value included frozen white leg shrimps, frozen chicken meat, and fresh or frozen fish, which accounted for 69% of top 10 exports (Table 15). The value of import onions, garlics, and fresh potatoes account for 93% of top 10 imports.

Table 15: Ban Prakop Customs House: Top 10 Export–Import Values in 2018

Rank	Export	Weight (kg)	Value ($ '000)	Import	Weight (kg)	Value ($' 000)
1	Frozen white leg shrimps	3,297,678	17,482	Onions, garlics	5,103,000	3,013
2	Frozen chicken meat	7,251,292	9,361	Fresh potatoes	550,000	158
3	Natural rubber	15,278,000	7,265	Conveyors or equipment used to contain goods made of plastics	173,679	72
4	Fresh or dried pineapples, guavas, mangoes, mangosteens	9,993,400	3,865	Live fish	88,800	57
5	Other fresh fruits	743,700	811	Coconuts	105,000	32
6	Fresh or frozen fish	902,800	678	Malt beer	25,073	21
7	Grist	124,600	173	Used clothes	16,706	13
8	Live cattle	6,060	92	Trailer or semi-trailer parts	5,690	9
9	Live fish	643,000	80	Diesel or semi-diesel engines	2,050	4
10	Brine shrimp eggs	1,071	64	Household products	9,650	4

Sources: Ban Prakop Customs House, 2019; Bank of Thailand. https://www.bot.or.th/App/BTWS_STAT/statistics/ReportPage.aspx?reportID=123&language=th (accessed 26 February 2020).

Tourism

The number of visitor arrivals at Hat Yai International Airport increased by 8.7% from $7.0 million in 2017 to $7.6 million in 2018 (Table 16). About 60% of these visitors are Thais. However, the number of Malaysian visitors has increased significantly by 15% compared to the increase in Thai domestic tourists at 5%. Hat Yai Airport is a Southern Thailand aviation hub with passenger traffic close to 5 million and flights of 9,000 in 2018.

Table 16: Number of Visitors to Songkhla via Hat Yai International Airport

Item	Number of Visitors (persons)		
	2017	2018[a]	Percent Change (%)
Visitors	7,025,573	7,635,378	8.68
Thais	4,396,474	4,609,816	4.85
Foreigners	2,629,099	3,025,562	15.08

[a] Preliminary.
Source: Ministry of Tourism and Sports, 2019.

Industrial Activities

The Songkhla Special Economic Zone (Songkhla SEZ) comprises four subdistricts in Sadao District: (i) Sadao subdistrict, (ii) Samnak Kham subdistrict, (iii) Samnak Taeo subdistrict, and (iv) Padang Besar subdistrict. The SEZ covers a total area of 552.3 square kilometers (km^2) (55,230 hectares). It is located not far from Sadao and Padang Besar BCPs and connects to Kedah and Perlis in Malaysia by road. The industrial estate in Songkhla SEZ will be in Samnak Kham subdistrict covering an area of 175.60 hectares, 2 km from Sadao checkpoint, and 35 km from Padang Besar checkpoint. It is next to Kanchanawanit road. The physical condition of the area consists of slope with water nearby and electricity accessible to the area.

As of 2019, there were 498 registered enterprises with investments of B6,054.37 million ($195.3 million) in the SEZ district. The number of registered enterprises investing in the Songkhla SEZ constitutes 4.9% of investments outside the SEZ. The investment value in the SEZ constitutes 5.3% of investment outside the zone. About 98% of businesses in the SEZ are SMEs engaged mainly in services such as Customs brokers, transport and loading and unloading of goods, and transport of passengers, as well as real estate.

The investment value of foreign shareholding in the SEZ is B1,459.95 million ($47.1 million) or 24.11% of the total investment value. The top three investors are Malaysia (97.09%), Spain (0.13%), and Libya (0.07%). Foreign investment's top five businesses include real estate, hygienic or pharmaceutical products from rubber, hotels, resorts, and condominiums.

Findings and Recommendations

The overall transport infrastructure in EC1 is in good condition. The transport system consists mostly of transport of agricultural produce and products from plantations that are brought to the factories and ultimately to domestic and foreign consumers through the Thailand–Malaysia borders. Most transport are through land and rail. The important transport system includes Songkhla Port, which transports goods between the south and the central plains of Thailand. Songkhla Port is a maritime gateway node that connects to GMS (Laem Chabang, Chonburi Province) and toward the Thai–Malaysian BCP to Penang Port.

Songkhla Port II needs to be established to link with Penang Port through a land bridge that will reduce the time and cost of transporting goods between the two ocean ports.

The Sadao BCP accounts for the highest share in Thailand–Malaysia border trade. It has been facing congestion due to the high volume of trade and tourists. The new Sadao BCP needs to link with Padang Besar to increase capacity for large-scale movement of passengers and cargoes.

The Padang Besar–Padang Besa BCP complements Sadao–Bukit Kayu Hitam. The Padang Besar border crossing is the gateway of transporting goods from Thailand to Malaysia via road and rail. Most goods are transported via Penang Port to other destination countries. There is great potential to increase the volume of trade at the Padang Besar border crossing on account of the rail transport as well as the transshipment and transit of goods at the border. Utilizing rail transport at Padang Besa or Padang Besar BCP and establishing a large Customs-controlled areas will facilitate container shipments to Penang Port.

Ban Prakop is a new border crossing with modern immigration, customs, quarantine, and security (ICQS) facilities and good roads on both sides of the border. It is an alternative import–export channel due to less traffic.

EC1 has multimodal connectivity covering roads, rail, ports, and airports together with SEZs, inland container depots (ICDs), and related facilities. To facilitate investment, trade, and tourism along the EC1 and with other corridors, these facilities must be developed and integrated based on standards and readiness.

Reconfiguration of Economic Corridor 1

Thailand's SEC development plan is seeking to promote and develop connectivity among tourist destinations along the coasts of the Andaman Sea and the Gulf of Thailand. This will be done by supporting the development of new inland tourist destinations and other high potential community attractions to create a tourist route network in Phuket, Phangnga, Krabi, Surat Thani (Ko Samui, Ko Pha-ngan, Ko Toa), Chumphon, and Nakhon Si Thammarat (Sichon and Khanom beaches). EC1 would connect to EC5 (Ranong and Phuket) to serve as the starting point for this tourism network offering world-class attractions and services.

The reconfiguration of EC1 in Thailand will include the provinces of Chumphon, Surat Thani, Phatthalung, which together with Songkhla and Nakhon Si Thammarat, will bring to five the number of Thailand participating provinces in the corridor (Map 5). The integration of these five provinces into a single corridor will connect the tourism routes and facilitate the tourists' movement between destinations in the Gulf of Thailand and the Andaman Sea. It will also expand the areas of cooperation in the agriculture and industry sectors by connecting agricultural products in the value chain of halal food processing in Indonesia and Malaysia. In addition, Thailand proposed to integrate the part of Extended EC1 (Pattani, Yala, and Narathiwat) to link with the eastern part of Malaysia on EC6 (Map 6). Therefore, the three southern border provinces have moved to EC6.

**Map 5: Southern Thailand–Northern Malaysia–North Sumatera Economic Corridor
(Reconfigured Economic Corridor 1)**

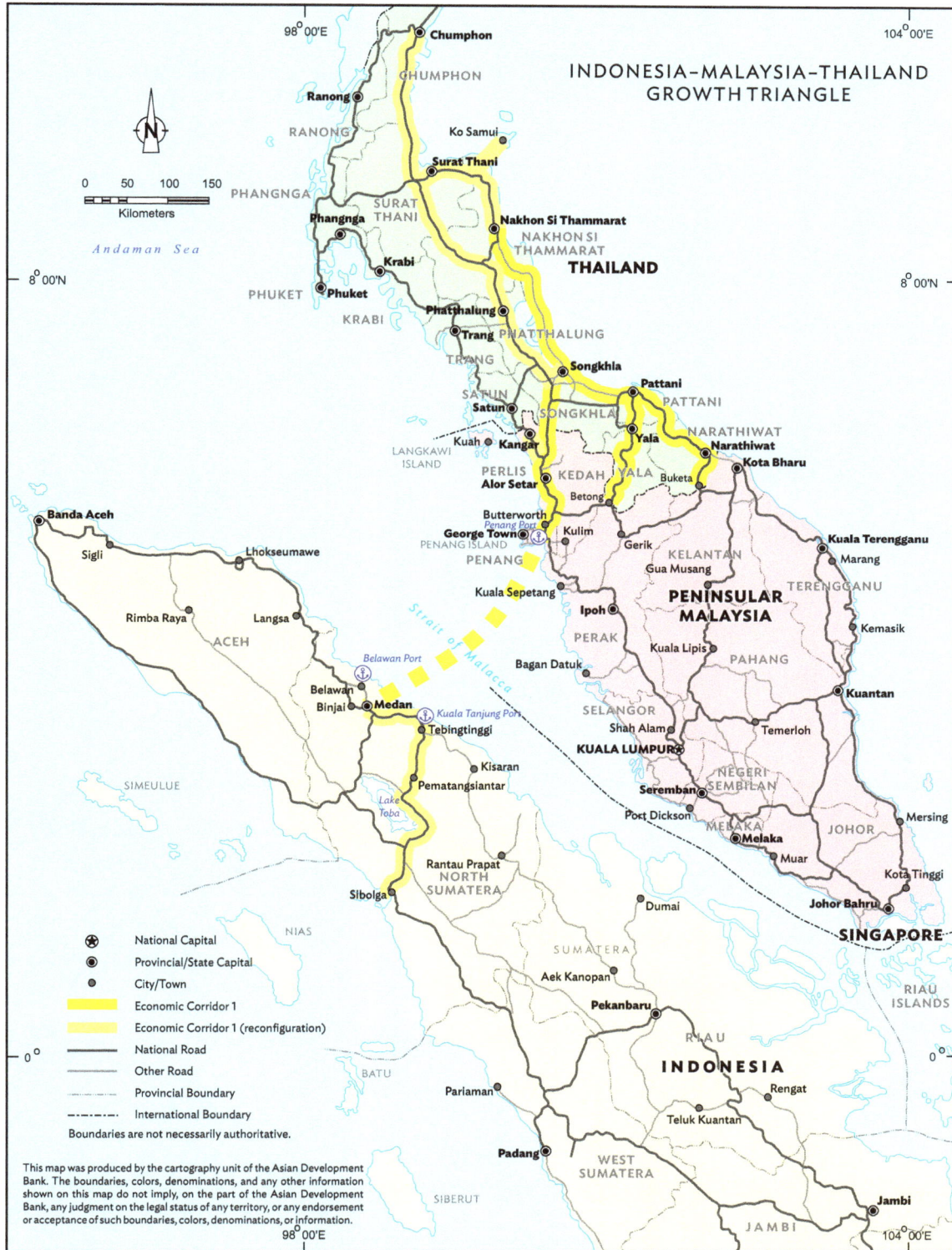

Source: Asian Development Bank.

Map 6: Southern Thailand–Northern Malaysia–North Sumatera Economic Corridor (Reconfigured Economic Corridor 1) - Thailand

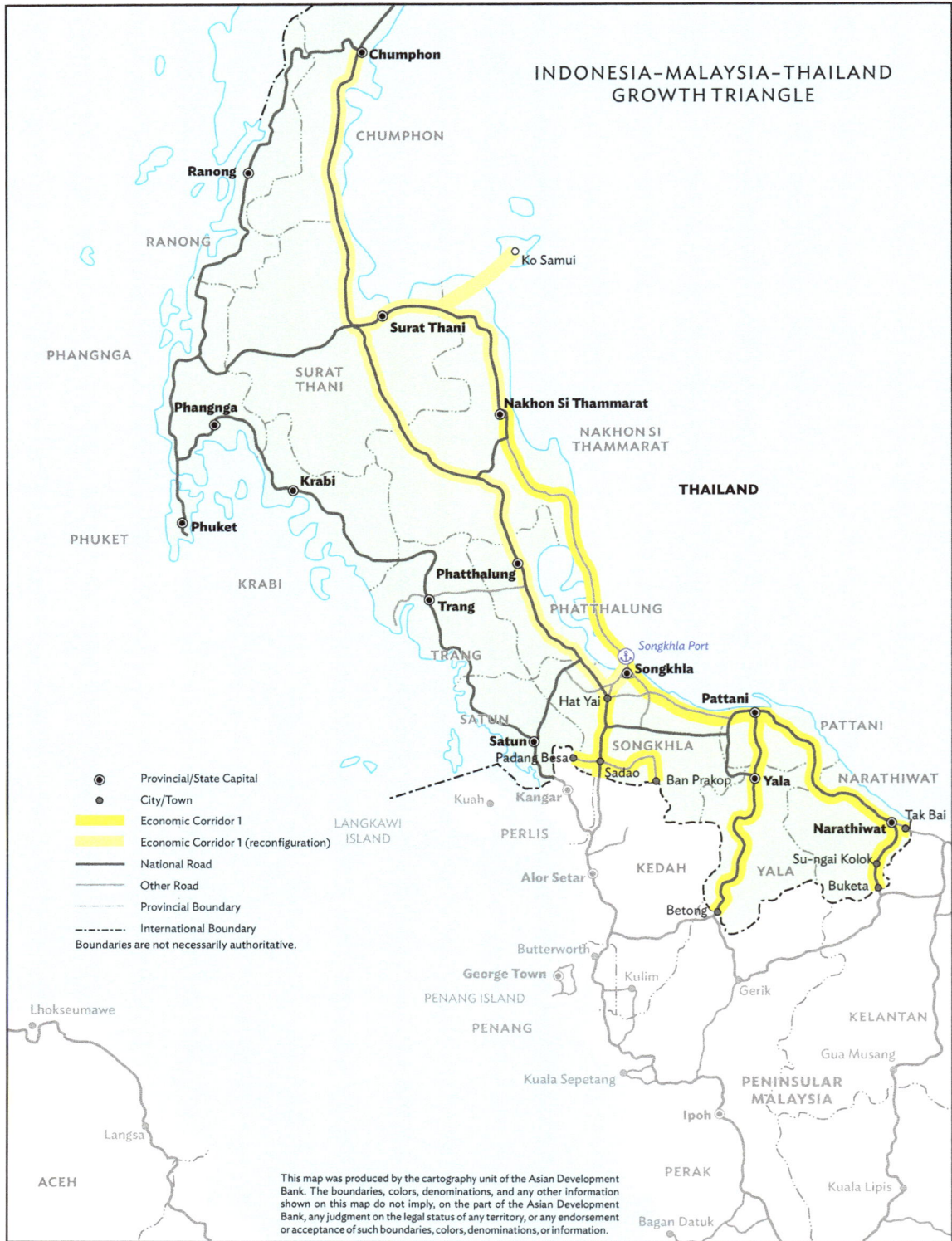

INDONESIA–MALAYSIA–THAILAND GROWTH TRIANGLE

Chumphon

CHUMPHON

Ranong

RANONG

Ko Samui

Surat Thani

SURAT THANI

Nakhon Si Thammarat

NAKHON SI THAMMARAT

PHANGNGA

Phangnga

THAILAND

Krabi

Phuket

PHUKET

KRABI

Phatthalung

Trang

PHATTHALUNG

TRANG

Songkhla Port

Songkhla

Hat Yai

Pattani

PATTANI

SATUN

Satun

SONGKHLA

Padang Besa

Kuah   Kangar   Sadao   Ban Prakop   Yala   NARATHIWAT

LANGKAWI ISLAND

PERLIS   Tak Bai

Narathiwat

Su-ngai Kolok

Buketa

Alor Setar   KEDAH   YALA

Betong

Butterworth

George Town   Kulim

PENANG ISLAND   Gerik

PENANG   KELANTAN

Lhokseumawe   Gua Musang

Kuala Sepetang   PENINSULAR MALAYSIA

Ipoh

Langsa

PERAK   Kuala Lipis

ACEH

Bagan Datuk

Legend:
- ◉ Provincial/State Capital
- ● City/Town
- ▬ Economic Corridor 1
- ▬ Economic Corridor 1 (reconfiguration)
- ── National Road
- ── Other Road
- ─·─ Provincial Boundary
- ─··─ International Boundary

Boundaries are not necessarily authoritative.

This map was produced by the cartography unit of the Asian Development Bank. The boundaries, colors, denominations, and any other information shown on this map do not imply, on the part of the Asian Development Bank, any judgment on the legal status of any territory, or any endorsement or acceptance of such boundaries, colors, denominations, or information.

Source: Asian Development Bank.

Complementary economic activities in EC1 include agriculture and agro-based industry, tourism, transport, trade and investment facilitation, and halal products value chain and services. Chumphon, Surat Thani, and Songkhla are the collective areas of agricultural products within the province and from adjacent provinces. These products are transported to processing facilities and distributed to domestic consumers or exported via Thai–Malaysian borders that connect to Songkhla Port and Laem Chabang Port and onward to the PRC and other export destinations. Chumphon, Surat Thani, and Songkhla are where most processing facilities are located for rubber and rubber wood and for seafood.

Indonesia and Malaysia have added states and provinces in EC1 according to their countries' development strategies. Indonesia has included three nodes in North Sumatera: (i) Kuala Tanjung Port and industrial zone, (ii) Sibolga Port and Sibolga City, and (iii) Lake Toba. Indonesia's strategy for EC1 aligns with the development of Sumatera Island that leverages on the ongoing construction of the Trans-Sumatera Toll Road, the planned expansion of ports and airports, and the establishment of industrial parks and SEZs. The focus is on the development of downstream products for agriculture, fisheries, and mining-based industries, and catalyzing export-oriented growth centers for more value added.

For Malaysia, there are no additional nodes in EC1. The existing nodes in the three states are well aligned with the development plans of national economic corridors in northern Malaysia. Major developments in the border areas in Bukit Kayu Hitam, Durian Burung, and Padang Besar will likely have significant impact on the economic activities in the corridor in the near to medium term.

Table 17 shows the EC1 existing and additional provinces and nodes by type.

Based on the additional provinces and nodes, **EC1 has been renamed Southern Thailand–Northern Malaysia–North Sumatera Economic Corridor**.

Table 17: Economic Corridor 1: Existing and Additional Provinces and Nodes, by Type

Province/State	Node	Type				
		CAP	COM	BCP	MGP	TOUR
INDONESIA						
North Sumatera	Belawan Port				✓	
	Medan	✓				
	Kuala Tanjung Port*		✓		✓	
	Sibolga*		✓		✓	
	Lake Toba*					✓
MALAYSIA						
Penang	Penang Port • Butterworth • George Town		✓		✓	✓
Kedah	Bukit Kayu Hitam		✓	✓		✓
	Durian Burung		✓	✓		
	Alor Setar	✓				
Perlis	Padang Besar		✓	✓		✓
	Kangar*	✓				
THAILAND						
Songkhla	Songkhla	✓				
	Songkhla Port*				✓	
	Hat Yai		✓			
	Sadao			✓		
	Padang Besa			✓		
	Ban Prakop			✓		
Nakhon Si Thammarat	Nakhon Si Thammarat	✓				
Chumphon*	Chumphon*	✓				
Surat Thani*	Surat Thani*	✓	✓			
	Ko Samui*					✓
Phatthalung	Phatthalung City	✓				
Pattani**	Pattani City	✓				
Yala**	Yala City	✓				
Narathiwat**	Narathiwat City	✓	✓			

BCP = border crossing point, CAP = capital, COM = commercial, EC = economic corridor, MGP = maritime gateway port, TOUR = tourism.
Notes:
* Denotes additional provinces and nodes.
** Pattani, Yala, and Narathiwat were part of the extended EC1 but these provinces have been integrated with the proposed route for EC6 to link with the eastern part of Malaysia.
Source: Study team.

Economic Corridor 2. The Strait of Malacca Economic Corridor

Overview

The Strait of Malacca Economic Corridor (EC2) is a coastal corridor connecting the Thai provinces of Trang and Satun with the Malaysian province of Perlis, and on to Port Klang, Penang, and Melaka along the western coast (Maps 7 and 8). The approach to connectivity is multimodal, with land and coastal linkages.

The proximity of this corridor to Sumatera's eastern coast along the Strait of Malacca offers potential for complementation along various stages of the production chain. The reconfigured EC2 can also serve as halal food hub since several terminals and centers are being planned along the corridor.

The main transport route for EC2 starts in Trang Province (Route 404/416) going to the border at Wang Prachan in Satun. From Wang Prachan, one route goes to Tammalang Port, which connects by land to Penang Port. Another goes to Padang Besa in Sadao across the border at Padang Besar in Perlis. An alternative route from Wang Prachan goes to Wang Kelian, also in Perlis. A third entry point from Thailand is at Betong, Yala at the border of Pengkalan Hulu in Perak. The BCPs in EC2 are

(i)   Wang Prachan (Satun)–Wang Kelian (Perlis),

(ii)   Padang Besa (Songkhla)–Padang Besar (Perlis), and

(iii)   Betong (Yala)–Pengkalan Hulu (Perak).

Existing Provinces and Nodes in Thailand

Trang and Satun are the provinces in the existing EC2. Trang City is a commercial center for business, agriculture, and tourism. Trang's GPP in 2018 was valued $1,229 million with the GPP per capita at $3,175. The provincial production structure ratio comprises the service sector (56.7%), the agriculture sector (27.5%), and the industry sector (15.7%) (Table 18).

Table 18: Socioeconomic Profile of Trang Province

Land Area	4,918 km²	**Population of Thailand**	66.41 million (2018)
GPP ($ million in constant prices)		Of which, in Trang	643,116 (0.97%)
2014	1,228.82	Urban population	116,453 (18.1%)
2018	1,229.13	Rural population	526,663 (81.9%)
Growth rate 2014–2018 (%)	0.01	**Population density**	
Share to GRP (%)	4.6	2005	122.4
Share to GDP (%)	0.37	2010	126.6
Rank in Southern Region	8	2018	130.8
GPP per capita, 2018 ($)	3,175	**Labor and Employment**	
Agriculture Sector (%)	27.5	Economically active population	381,628
Service Sector (%)	56.7	Employed	377,034 (98.8%)
Industry Sector (%)	15.7	Unemployed	4,595 (1.2%)

GDP = gross domestic product, GPP = gross provincial product, GRP = gross regional product, km² = square kilometer.
Source: Office of the National Economic and Social Development Board, 2019.

**Map 7: Strait of Malacca Economic Corridor
(Economic Corridor 2)**

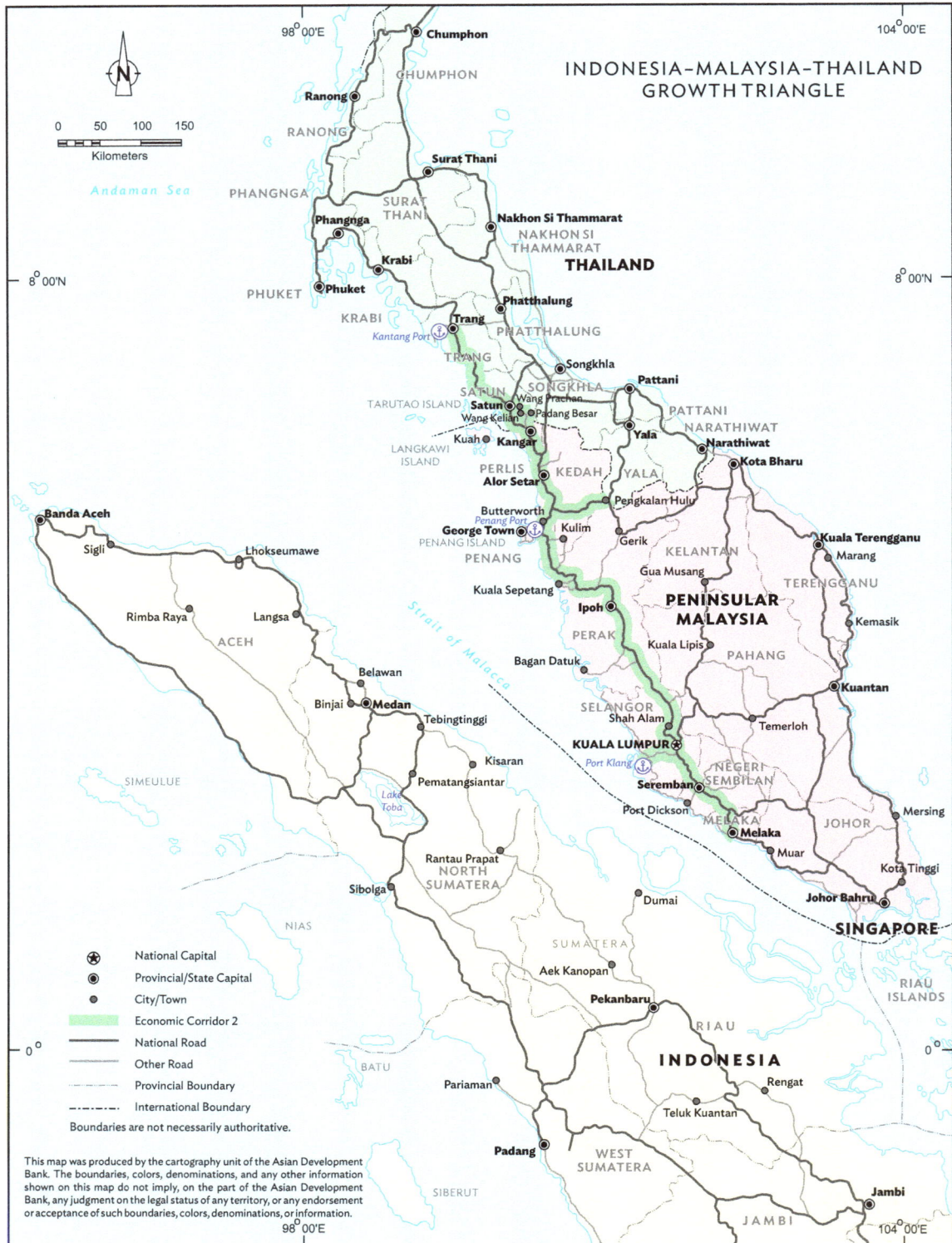

INDONESIA–MALAYSIA–THAILAND
GROWTH TRIANGLE

98°00'E

104°00'E

N

0   50   100   150
Kilometers

Andaman Sea

8°00'N

8°00'N

Chumphon

CHUMPHON

Ranong

RANONG

Surat Thani

SURAT
THANI

Phangnga

PHANGNGA

Nakhon Si Thammarat

NAKHON SI
THAMMARAT

THAILAND

Krabi

Phuket

PHUKET

KRABI

Phatthalung

PHATTHALUNG

Trang

TRANG

Kantang Port

Songkhla

SATUN

SONGKHLA

Wang Prachan

Pattani

Satun

TARUTAO ISLAND

Wang Kelian

Padang Besar

PATTANI

NARATHIWAT

Yala

Kuah

Kangar

YALA

Narathiwat

LANGKAWI
ISLAND

PERLIS

KEDAH

Kota Bharu

Alor Setar

Pengkalan Hulu

Butterworth

Penang Port

George Town

Kulim

PENANG ISLAND

Gerik

KELANTAN

Kuala Terengganu

Marang

TERENGGANU

PENANG

Banda Aceh

Sigli

Lhokseumawe

Kuala Sepetang

Ipoh

PEINSULAR
MALAYSIA

Gua Musang

Kemasik

Rimba Raya

Langsa

ACEH

PERAK

Kuala Lipis

PAHANG

Bagan Datuk

Belawan

Binjai

Medan

Tebingtinggi

Kuantan

SELANGOR

Shah Alam

Temerloh

Kisaran

KUALA LUMPUR

SIMEULUE

Pematangsiantar

Lake
Toba

Port Klang

Seremban

NEGERI
SEMBILAN

Port Dickson

Rantau Prapat

NORTH
SUMATERA

MELAKA

Mersing

Sibolga

Muar

JOHOR

Melaka

Kota Tinggi

Dumai

Johor Bahru

NIAS

SUMATERA

SINGAPORE

Aek Kanopan

RIAU
ISLANDS

0°

0°

Pekanbaru

RIAU

BATU

INDONESIA

Pariaman

Rengat

Teluk Kuantan

Padang

WEST
SUMATERA

SIBERUT

Jambi

JAMBI

98°00'E

104°00'E

Legend:
- National Capital
- Provincial/State Capital
- City/Town
- Economic Corridor 2
- National Road
- Other Road
- Provincial Boundary
- International Boundary

Boundaries are not necessarily authoritative.

This map was produced by the cartography unit of the Asian Development Bank. The boundaries, colors, denominations, and any other information shown on this map do not imply, on the part of the Asian Development Bank, any judgment on the legal status of any territory, or any endorsement or acceptance of such boundaries, colors, denominations, or information.

Strait of Malacca

Source: Asian Development Bank.

**Map 8: Strait of Malacca Economic Corridor
(Economic Corridor 2) – Thailand**

INDONESIA–MALAYSIA–THAILAND
GROWTH TRIANGLE

Chumphon

CHUMPHON

Ranong

Andaman Sea

RANONG

PHANGNGA

Surat Thani

SURAT
THANI

Phangnga

Nakhon Si Thammarat

NAKHON SI
THAMMARAT

Krabi

THAILAND

PHUKET

Phuket

KRABI

Phatthalung

PHATTHALUNG

Kantang Port Trang

TRANG

Songkhla

SATUN

Pattani

PATTANI

Satun   Wang Prachan

SONGKHLA

Wang Kelian
Kuah   Kangar

Yala

Narathiwat

LANGKAWI
ISLAND

PERLIS

NARATHIWAT

Alor Setar

KEDAH

YALA

Lhokseumawe

Butterworth

George Town

Kulim

Gerik

KELANTAN

PENANG ISLAND

PENANG

Gua Musang

Kuala Sepetang

PENINSULAR
MALAYSIA

Langsa

Ipoh

ACEH

PERAK

Kuala Lipis

Bagan Datuk

Legend:
- ◉ Provincial/State Capital
- ◦ City/Town
- Economic Corridor 2
- National Road
- Other Road
- Provincial Boundary
- International Boundary

Boundaries are not necessarily authoritative.

This map was produced by the cartography unit of the Asian Development Bank. The boundaries, colors, denominations, and any other information shown on this map do not imply, on the part of the Asian Development Bank, any judgment on the legal status of any territory, or any endorsement or acceptance of such boundaries, colors, denominations, or information.

Source: Asian Development Bank.

Satun has a major reservation forest, fertile mangroves, and world-renowned marine ecotourism. The coastal area is suitable for deepwater fishery operation, including marine aquaculture. Satun's GPP in 2018 was valued $643 million with the GPP per capita at $3,327. The provincial production structure ratio comprises the service sector (52.7%), the agricultural sector (36.7%) and the industry sector (10.6%) (Table 19). The important nodes in Satun are Wang Prachan, Tammalang Port, and Kantang Port.

(i)   **Wang Prachan**. Wang Prachan is a joint border commercial development and linked to nearby ecotourism areas and accommodates trade between Satun and Perlis.

(ii)   **Tammalang Port**. Tammalang Port is a major tourist port connecting Thailand and Malaysia. It provides ferry service to Langkawi Island, Malaysia. Tourism is mostly a 1-day trip. Moreover, there are other tourism routes such as Tammalang–Lipe, and Tammalang–Tarutao Islands. There is high potential to initiate a new Thailand–Indonesia tourist route from Tammalang to Belawan in the future.

(iii) **Kantang Port**. Kantang Port is an important port for the export of rubber and rubber products but it can only accommodate small vessels with its limited depth. Connectivity of Kantang Port by rail to the Thung Song Cargo Distribution Center—the logistic hub of Nakhon Si Thammarat (EC1) and Southern Thailand—will enhance the transport route for goods in Southern Thailand. Nakhon Si Thammarat, Thung Song Station is the junction for the southern main line (Bangkok–Padang Besa–Su-ngai Kolok) and the southern branch line to Trang Province and Kantang Port.

Table 19: Socioeconomic Profile of Satun Province

Land Area	2,479 km²	Population of Thailand	66.41 million (2018)
GPP ($ million in constant prices)		Of which, in Satun	321,574 (0.48%)
2014	690.12	Urban population	63,517 (19.75%)
2018	643.66	Rural population	258,057 (80.25%)
Growth rate 2014-2018 (%)	–1.73	Population density	
Share to GRP (%)	2.43	2005	112.09
Share to GDP (%)	0.19	2010	119.87
Rank in Southern Region	12	2018	129.72
GPP per capita, 2018 ($)	3,327	Labor and Employment	
Agriculture Sector (%)	36.73	Economically active population	148,003
Service Sector (%)	52.70	Employed	144,561 (97.67%)
Industry Sector (%)	10.57	Unemployed	3,441 (2.33%)

GDP = gross domestic product, GPP = gross provincial product, GRP = gross regional product, km² = square kilometer.
Source: Office of the National Economic and Social Development Board, 2019.

Status of Physical Connectivity

Road Connectivity

The route of Trang–Satun–Strait of Malacca (EC2) in Thailand is divided into three sections: Trang Mueang District–Satun Mueang District, Satun Mueang District–Wang Prachan Customs Checkpoint, and Satun Mueang District–Tammalang Port. The road surface in all three sections is smooth for the entire section. The route is safe, equipped with traffic signs, traffic lines, complete and undamaged safety equipment, curved guideposts, and complete guardrail in good condition. The details of physical status and conditions of each route are as in Table 20.

Table 20: Economic Corridor 2: Start and End Points in Thailand

Start Point	End Point	Route	Distance (km)	Traffic Lanes	Road Classification	Road Condition
Trang	Satun	404/406	148	2/4	Class I	Good
Satun	Wang Prachan Border	406/4184	40	2/4	Class I/Class II	Good
Satun	Tammalang Pier	406	11.5	2/4	I	Good

km = kilometer.
Source: Compiled by the author.

Rail Connectivity

There are rail links between Port Klang, Perak, and Songkhla as well as a land bridge from Port Klang extending all the way to Hat Yai. The construction of a new bridge connecting Satun and Perlis will further enhance land connectivity along the Andaman Sea coast from Tammalang in Satun to Perlis in Malaysia by shortening the trip from Bangkok to Padang Besar, Bukit Kayu Hitam, and Kedah and will stimulate economic activities in the local community.

Within Thailand, rail connectivity along EC2 is limited. There is rail connectivity between Chumphon and Satun but long-distance rail service to and from Trang Station is not frequent.

Cross-Border Nodes

The Wang Prachan BCP is a Customs House via land situated at Kilometer 22 on the provincial Highway 4184, Khuan Don District, Satun. The opposite border in Malaysia is from Wang Kelian in Perlis, Malaysia. It covers the area of 49 *rai*[6] and it is open from 7:00 a.m. to 6:00 p.m. There is currently an international cross-border market based on an agreement between Satun and Perlis.

Roads leading to Thailand BCPs at Wang Prachan and Padang Besa are in good condition. Two important projects between Thailand and Malaysia involving the border nodes are

(i)   the joint initiative for the development of Customs checkpoint at Wang Kelian and Wang Prachan involving the upgrading of the Customs House, and establishment of low-rise commercial zones linked to nearby ecotourism tourism areas and commodities trade; and

(ii) the construction of a new bridge connecting Satun and Perlis along the Andaman Sea coast to accommodate the increase in transport demand resulting from economic growth.

Maritime Connectivity

The key maritime gateway ports in EC2 are Tammalang Port (Satun), Kantang Port (Trang), Port Klang (Selangor), Penang Port (Penang), Tanjung Bruas Port (Melaka), and Lumut Port. These ports are accessible by good roads from urban and commercial centers in the corridor.

---

[6]   *Rai* is a Thai unit of area equal to 1,600 m².

In Thailand, the main port in EC2 is Tammalang Port located at Tammalang Subdistrict, Mueang District, Satun. It is currently a pier for cruises and outgoing pier to Malaysia. It provides ferry service to Langkawi Island, Malaysia, with 1 hour travel time. The service provides six ferries a day both incoming and outgoing from 8:30 a.m. to 4:30 p.m. Tourism is mostly 1-day trip. Tourism is possible all year-round due to the range of islands serving as monsoon defense range. Other tourism routes are Penang–Belawan, Penang–Langkawi (operated by Malaysians) and Langkawi–Lipe (operated by Thais).

The goods passing through the Customs port are divided into (i) those exported to Langkawi Island, mostly fresh food; and (ii) those exported to Malaysia. The ships used for transport are midsized, modified ships. There are no containerized goods passing through this port. However, Tammalang Port also has a yacht pier, but which has not been open for service for over 20 years due to the shallow channel.

Trade

Thailand's border trade with Malaysia was driven mostly by imports that grew faster than exports on average over 2015–2018 (Table 21). Thailand's trade with Malaysia at the border of Padang Besa contributed 12.5% to Thailand's total border trade in 2018. Border trade at Wang Prachan and Betong is small, at less than 1%. Imports grew at an average of 16.84% at Padang Besa, and 62% for Wang Prachan over 2015–2018, overtaking exports, which grew much slower.

Table 21: Economic Corridor 2: Thailand's Border Trade with Malaysia

Item	Padang Besa	Wang Prachan	Betong
Average total trade 2015–2018 ($ '000)	5,339,250	7,750	99,740
Share to Thailand's total border trade, 2018 (%)	12.46	0.02	0.23
Average growth rate of exports (%)	0.12	(15.66)	0.92
Average growth rate of imports (%)	16.84	62.24	(7.95)

( ) = negative.
Source: Padang Besa, Wang Prachan, Betong Customs Houses, 2019.

The Wang Prachan–Wang Kelian border between Satun and Perlis has a free trade area on both sides of the border. Since December 2008, there has been a 1 km visa-free access on either side of the border crossing for visitors to the bazaar. It is a market for commodities and local products popular among the locals that visit in large number on Sundays. In 2019, the import value recorded at the border was only $5.71 million and no export data was recorded at the Wang Prachan BCP. There is also a joint development at the border of Wang Prachan–Wang Kelian that will establish a Customs check point providing a one-stop service.

Tourism

Satun is a major tourist hub connecting Thailand and the Malaysian island of Langkawi via ferry services. Other tourism routes include Tammalang–Lipe, and Tammalang–Tarutao Islands. There is high potential to initiate a new Thailand–Indonesia tourist route from Tammalang to Belawan in the future. In 2018, 1.05 million tourists visited Satun, around 90% of which were domestic tourists. Trang City has many Chinese historical attractions and most visitors stay in town to enjoy Muslim and Chinese cuisine and scenery.

**Map 9: Andaman Sea–Strait of Malacca Economic Corridor
(Reconfigured Economic Corridor 2)**

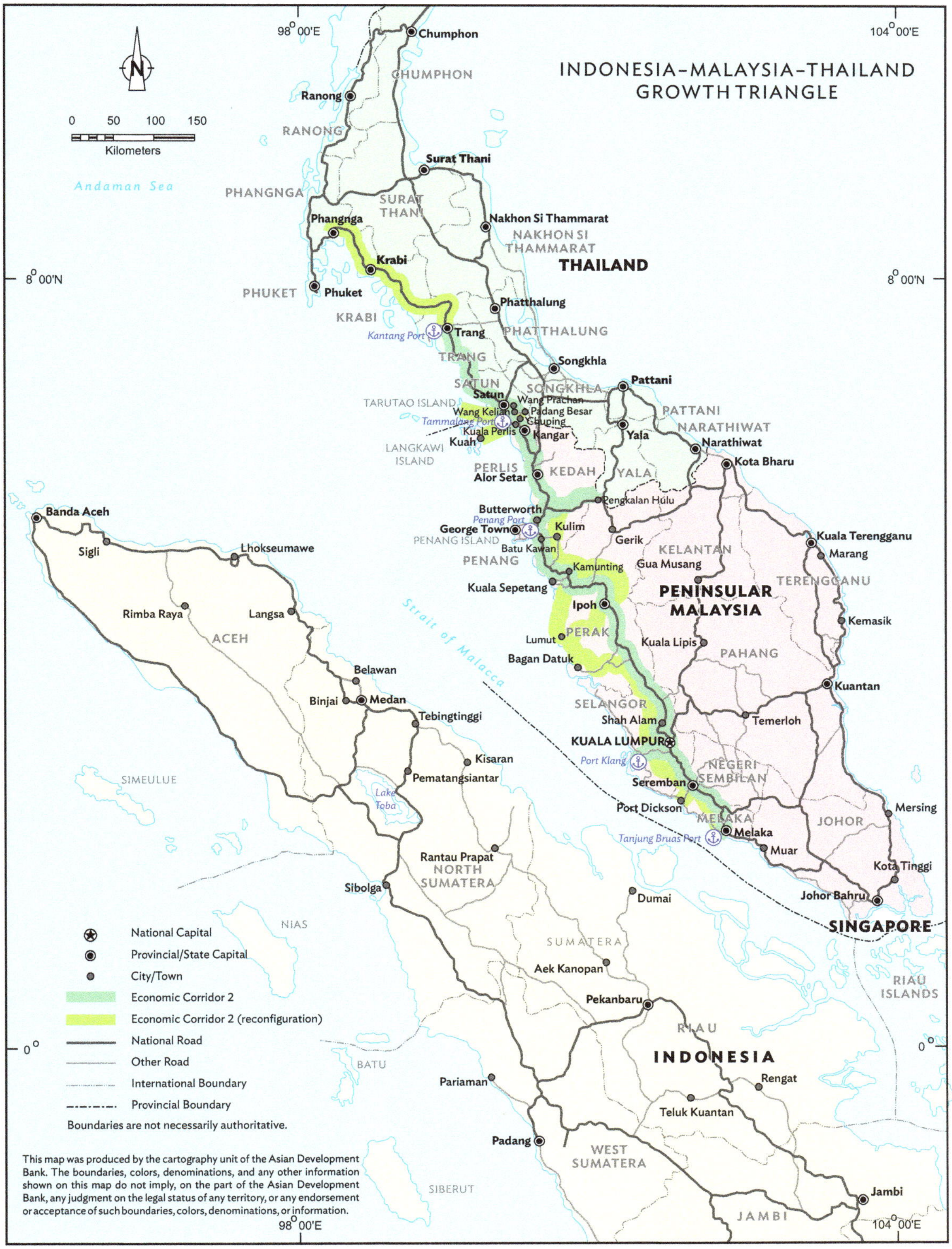

Source: Asian Development Bank.

**Map 10: Andaman Sea–Strait of Malacca Economic Corridor
(Reconfigured Economic Corridor 2) - Thailand**

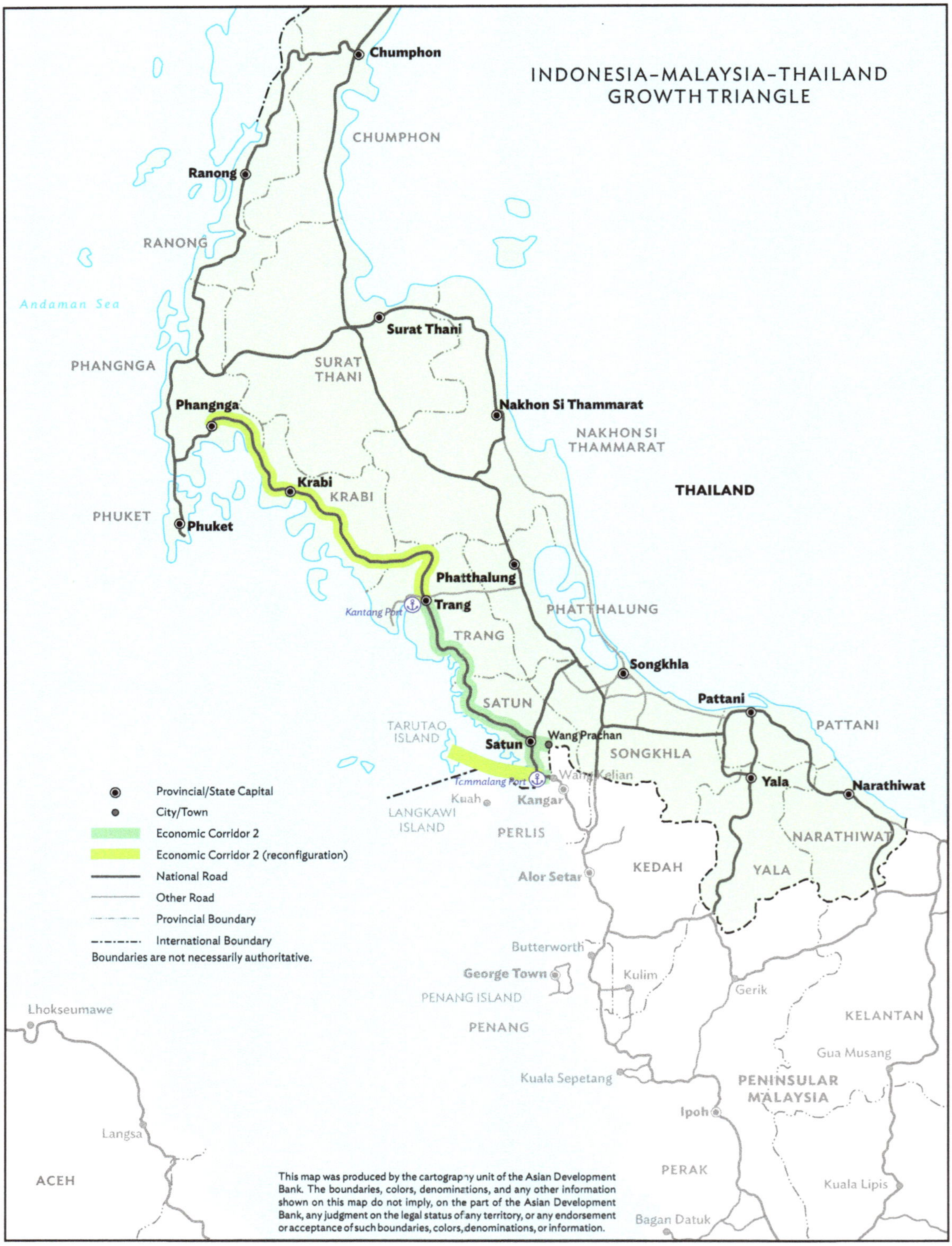

INDONESIA–MALAYSIA–THAILAND
GROWTH TRIANGLE

Chumphon

CHUMPHON

Ranong

RANONG

Andaman Sea

PHANGNGA

Surat Thani

SURAT
THANI

Phangnga

Nakhon Si Thammarat

NAKHON SI
THAMMARAT

PHUKET

Krabi

KRABI

Phuket

THAILAND

Phatthalung

Kantang Port   Trang

PHATTHALUNG

TRANG

Songkhla

SATUN

Pattani

TARUTAO
ISLAND

Satun   Wang Prachan

PATTANI

Tammalang Port   Wang Kelian   SONGKHLA

Kuah   Kangar

Yala

Narathiwat

LANGKAWI
ISLAND

PERLIS

KEDAH

YALA

NARATHIWAT

Alor Setar

Butterworth

George Town

PENANG ISLAND

Kulim

Gerik

KELANTAN

PENANG

Gua Musang

Kuala Sepetang

PENINSULAR
MALAYSIA

Ipoh

Lhokseumawe

Langsa

ACEH

PERAK

Kuala Lipis

Bagan Datuk

● Provincial/State Capital
● City/Town
▨ Economic Corridor 2
▬ Economic Corridor 2 (reconfiguration)
— National Road
— Other Road
—·— Provincial Boundary
—··— International Boundary
Boundaries are not necessarily authoritative.

This map was produced by the cartography unit of the Asian Development Bank. The boundaries, colors, denominations, and any other information shown on this map do not imply, on the part of the Asian Development Bank, any judgment on the legal status of any territory, or any endorsement or acceptance of such boundaries, colors, denominations, or information.

Source: Asian Development Bank.

Findings and Recommendations

The main agricultural products of Trang and Satun are palm oil, rubber, and fruits. The products are sent to processing factories in Chumphon, Surat Thani, and Songkhla. Satun's coastal area is also suitable for deepwater fishery and marine aquaculture. Marine aquaculture products are processed in factories in Satun.

Overall, transport systems by road, rail, and ports in EC2 are in good condition. Kantang Port is the only port that connects the southern railway system at Thong Song Cargo Distribution Center (CDC) in Nakhon Si Thammarat. It transports bulk goods and containerized goods. Major exports include rubber, ribbed smoked sheet (RSS), and processed rubber wood that are shipped to Penang Port for further destinations. Kantang Port has a high potential to become a major gateway for exporting cargoes to Port Klang in Malaysia and other ports in Indonesia.

Connectivity in EC2 can be further enhanced by

(i)   connecting tourist destinations along the coasts of the Andaman Sea both by land and by sea;

(ii)   utilizing the route for transport of goods, both via land and rail, to Kantang Port (rail from Thong Song CDC in Nakhon Si Thammarat in EC1);

(iii)   utilizing the route of tourism and transport of goods via sea between Tammalang Port to islands in Thailand, Malaysia, and Indonesia; and

(iv)   initiating multimodal transport through ports in Satun to Aceh and Belawan (roll-on, roll-off [Ro-Ro] ferry service to be pioneered between Belawan–Penang–Satun).

Reconfiguration of Economic Corridor 2

To support Thailand's strategy for the southern provinces, EC2 was extended northward to include Phangnga, Krabi. Therefore, the EC2 in Thailand will consist of Phangnga, Krabi, Trang, and Satun (Map 10). The objective is to facilitate tourist movement from Phuket, Krabi, and Phangnga into Trang and Satun. This will develop land and sea connectivity along the Andaman Sea coast for tourism and pave the way to connect EC2 and EC5. Krabi is a commercial and tourism node. If Krabi connects tourism and tourists along the coasts of the Andaman Sea from Ranong, Phangnga, Phuket, Krabi, Trang, and Satun, it can be a well-integrated tourism route in the EC2 onward to Malaysia and Indonesia.

Moreover, Tarutao National Park (island) is a tourist attraction because of its remoteness from the main tourist areas. There are many bays, both small and large, with beautiful beaches. It was also listed as one of the original ASEAN Heritage Parks and Reserves by the United Nations Educational, Scientific and Cultural Organization (UNESCO) in 1984. Tarutao can be reached by yacht and hired ferry.

The expansion of EC2 will also strengthen the domestic and cross-border palm oil and rubber value chain. Palm oil, rubber, and fruits produced in EC2 will supply to processing factories in Chumphon, Surat Thani, and Songkhla in EC1.

For Malaysia, the additional nodes in the reconfigured EC2 are (i) Pengkalan Hulu, Kamunting, Lumut, and Ipoh in Perak; (ii) Batu Kawan in Penang; (iii) Kuah and Langkawi in Kedah; and (iv) Tanjung Bruas Port in Melaka. Malaysia's strategy[7] for EC2 aligns with the development strategy for the Northern Corridor Economic Region to leverage good physical connectivity and regional trade networks with the development of core industry clusters for the region to achieve a world-class economic status by 2025. In reconfiguring EC2, Malaysia added new nodes at Chuping Valley, Kuala Perlis, Kamunting, Lumut, Batu Kawan, Kuah, Tanjung Bruas Port, Port Dickson, and Seremban, in addition to the existing nodes. These nodes will widen the connectivity with the existing nodes to achieve seamless connectivity and serve as growth nodes for the state's transition to a high-income economy and narrow regional disparities in the EC2.

Table 22 shows the EC2 existing and additional provinces and nodes by type.

Because of the inclusion of Thailand provinces along the Andaman Sea, **EC2 has been renamed Andaman Sea–Strait of Malacca Economic Corridor** (Maps 9 and 10).

Table 22: Economic Corridor 2: Existing and Additional Provinces and Nodes, by Type

Province/State	Node	Type				
		CAP	COM	BCP	MGP	TOUR
MALAYSIA						
Perlis	Wang Kelian			✓		✓
	Padang Besar			✓		✓
	Chuping Valley*		✓			
	Kuala Perlis*		✓			
Perak	Pengkalan Hulu			✓		✓
	Kamunting*		✓			
	Lumut*		✓			
Penang	Penang Port				✓	✓
	• Butterworth					
	• George Town					
	Batu Kawan*		✓			
Selangor	Port Klang				✓	✓
Kedah	Kuah*				✓	✓
	Langkawi					✓
Melaka	Melaka City	✓				✓
	Tanjung Bruas Port (Port of Melaka)*				✓	
Negeri Sembilan	Port Dickson*		✓		✓	✓
	Seremban*	✓	✓			
THAILAND						
Krabi*	Krabi City*	✓	✓			✓
Phangnga*	Phangnga City*	✓	✓			
Trang	Trang City	✓	✓			
	Kantang Port				✓	
Satun	Satun City	✓	✓			
	Wang Prachan			✓		
	Tammalang Port*				✓	✓
	Tarutao Island*					✓

BCP = border crossing point, CAP = capital, COM = commercial, MGP=maritme gateway port, TOUR = tourism.
Note: * denotes additional provinces and nodes.
Source: Study team.

7   A. R. Anuar. 2023. *Review and Assessment of the Indonesia–Malaysia–Thailand Growth Triangle Economic Corridors: Malaysia Country Report.* Manila: Asian Development Bank.

Economic Corridor 5. The Ranong–Phuket–Aceh Economic Corridor

Overview

The Ranong–Phuket–Aceh Economic Corridor (EC5) is mainly a maritime corridor linking ports in the northern part of Sumatera (mainly Ulee Lheue and Malahayati) with Phuket Port in Southern Thailand along its western coast facing the Andaman Sea, with the aim of exploiting tourism potentials. In Sumatera, Aceh Province is part of the corridor and Banda Aceh, the capital, and Sabang (located in the adjacent We Island) are the gateway and tourism nodes, respectively.

Ranong and Phuket are the two Thailand provinces in EC5. Ranong Port is a cargo and container port and is the main maritime gateway in the Andaman Sea connecting to trade routes with South Asia, the Middle East, Europe, and Africa. Phuket Port is mainly a pier for goods. Recently, cruise ships have made regular calls to the port, which has led to plans to develop Phuket as a homeport for cruises. Phuket also serves as a connecting route to South Asia, the Middle East, and Africa.

Existing Provinces and Nodes in Thailand

Ranong city is a gateway to Myanmar and serves as a major fishing and trading port. Ranong is famous for its hot springs, where various first-class hotels cater to visitors. Moreover, it serves as a commercial town for locals and nearby towns in Myanmar.

Ranong's GPP in 2018 was valued at $597.19 million with the GPP per capita at $3,217. The highest production structure ratio was service valued at $431 million (49.80%), followed by agriculture valued at $355 million (40.96%), and industry, valued at $80 million (9.24%) (Table 23).

Table 23: Socioeconomic Profile of Ranong Province

Land Area	3,298 km²	Population of Thailand	66.41 million (2018)
GPP ($ million in constant prices)		Of which, in Ranong	191,868 (0.29%)
2014	534.33	Urban population	31,977 (16.67%)
2018	597.19	Rural population	159,891 (83.33%)
Growth rate 2014-2018 (%)	2.82	Population density	
Share to GRP (%)	2.25	2005	54.01
Share to GDP (%)	0.18	2010	55.51
Rank in Southern Region	14	2018	58.18
GPP per capita, 2018 ($)	3,217	Labor and Employment	
Agriculture Sector (%)	40.96	Economically active population	133,216
Service Sector (%)	49.80	Employed	130,864 (98.23%)
Industry Sector (%)	9.24	Unemployed	2,352 (1.77%)

GDP = gross domestic product, GPP = gross provincial product, GRP = gross regional product, km² = square kilometer.
Source: Office of the National Economic and Social Development Board, 2019.

Phuket is a world-class tourism destination, the biggest island in Thailand and surrounded with beautiful islands and beaches. Over 10 million visitors visit Phuket every year by land, air, cruise, and yacht. Phuket's GPP 2018 valued at $5,021 million was the highest GPP per capita in the southern region, at $12,489. Phuket's economy relies heavily on service sector (especially, accommodation and food services), which makes up over 90% of its total GPP; followed by the agriculture sector, (2.67%) and the industry sector (2.89%) (Table 24).

Moreover, Phuket Island is developing into an international marina hub. Yacht visits have been exponentially increasing over a decade. In 2018, over 1,500 yachts visited Phuket Island and cruise ships dock regularly at Phuket Deep Seaport every year. Phuket has a high potential to become a tourism hub and distribute tourists to the nearby provinces and states along the EC2.

Table 24: Socioeconomic Profile of Phuket Province

Land Area	543 km²	Population of Thailand	66.41 million (2018)
GPP ($ million in constant prices)		Of which, in Phuket	410,211 (0.62%)
2014	3,582.63	Urban population	272,860 (66.52%)
2018	5,021.26	Rural population	137,351 (33.48%)
Growth rate 2014–2018 (%)	8.81	Population density	
Share to GRP (%)	18.93	2005	538.20
Share to GDP (%)	1.52	2010	635.48
Rank in Southern Region	2	2018	740.72
GPP per capita, 2018 ($)	12,489	**Labor and Employment**	
Agriculture Sector (%)	2.67	Economically active population	321,949
Service Sector (%)	94.44	Employed	306,392 (95.17%)
Industry Sector (%)	2.89	Unemployed	15,556 (4.83%)

GDP = gross domestic product, GPP = gross provincial product, GRP = gross regional product, km² = square kilometer.
Source: Office of the National Economic and Social Development Board, 2019.

Status of Physical Connectivity

Road Connectivity

The route along the Ranong–Phuket–Aceh Economic Corridor (EC5) in Thailand starts at Mueang District, Ranong, and ends at Mueang District, Phuket with a distance of 305 km (Maps 11 and 12). The route passes a wildlife sanctuary (Khlong Nakha Wildlife Sanctuary) and a national park (Khao Lak–Lam Ru National Park) using Highway 4 as main route. From the city of Ranong to Ngao Subdistrict, Mueang District, Ranong, the highway has four traffic lanes. But the route from there to over 250 km on Highways 401, 4090, 4240, and 4 until the intersection of Kok Loi Subdistrict, Takua Thung District, Phangnga will be a highway with two traffic lanes. The remaining section of the route will be Highway 402 heading to Phuket municipality with four traffic lanes. The road surface is smooth in the entire section. The route is safe, equipped with traffic signs, traffic lines, complete and undamaged safety equipment, curved guideposts, and complete guardrail in good condition. At present, Ranong Rural Roads Office has extended the entire route from Ranong to Phuket to four traffic lanes. It is expected that the construction will be finished in 2024.

**Map 11: Ranong–Phuket–Aceh Economic Corridor
(Economic Corridor 5)**

Source: Asian Development Bank.

Map 12: Ranong–Phuket–Aceh Economic Corridor
(Economic Corridor 5) - Thailand

Source: Asian Development Bank.

Maritime Connectivity

Apart from land, there is also maritime connectivity between Ranong and Phuket. The main ports in EC5 consist of Ranong Port and Phuket Deep Sea Port with the following features.

Ranong Port. Ranong Port is Thailand's principal Indian Ocean Port. It is on the east side of the estuary of Kraburi River, Pak Nam Subdistrict, Mueang District, Ranong with an area of 50.40 hectares. It is the main port on the Andaman Sea coast designed to connect to the trade route with countries in South Asia, the Middle East, Europe, and Africa. At present, Ranong Port can accommodate cargo ships and containers of 12,000 deadweight tons.

The Port Authority of Thailand, which supervises Ranong Port, has signed a memorandum of understanding with Navayuga Container Terminal and Krishna Patnam Port, India. The port–to–port cooperation has the objective of strengthening cooperation between the two ports in the areas of exchange of information, news on port management, port internal operation, promotion of marketing and investment in business related to port operation, information technology systems, communication and linkage of port networks, and promotion of industries related to port business. The duration of the cooperation is from 2019 to 2022.

Phuket Deep Sea Port. Phuket Deep Sea Port is on the Andaman Sea coast on the southeast of Phuket Island. Although Phuket Deep Sea Port has been designed mainly as a pier for goods, currently, more cruises have come to use the services on a continuous basis and the trend is up every year. Because of this, there is a plan to develop Phuket Port from a port of call to a homeport of call to accommodate large cruises and encouraging them to dock. Phuket is a popular tourist destination with a huge potential to attract more tourists from South Asia, the Middle East, Africa, and Europe.

Air Linkages

Thailand's airports in the Ranong–Phuket–Aceh Economic Corridor (EC5) consist of Ranong Airport and Phuket International Airport. Ranong Airport services only domestic flights provided by Nok Air and Thai AirAsia. In contrast, Phuket International Airport (IATA: HKT) is the third-busiest airport in the country, after Suvarnabhumi Airport and Don Mueang International Airport. It can accommodate 20 flights per hour, 5.1 million passengers per year, and the transport of 24,000 tons of goods per year. Currently, Phuket International Airport can accommodate passengers from 25 countries worldwide, serviced by 59 airlines operating international routes.

Air connectivity in EC5 is limited. There are no direct flights between Ranong and Phuket airports with Aceh airports and vice versa. Flights to these destinations are through the capital cities. Phuket International Airport has direct flights to Kuala Lumpur but none to Aceh or other parts of Indonesia.

Trade

Maritime trade links in EC5 ports have not developed and there has been very limited trade between Ranong and Phuket with Aceh. Thailand's links with Aceh are mostly in passenger ferry services. There are no commercial shipping routes for cargo from Malahayati Port (Aceh) to Phuket and Ranong Port. The port in Aceh that trades actively with Thailand is Meulaboh Port located in the western part of Aceh (and not part of EC5), which has become the main trade gateway for coal exports (more than 90%) to Thailand. Imports from Thailand go through the port in Arun Lhokseumawe.

Tourism

Phuket is a world-class tourist destination. In 2018, 10 million foreign tourists and 4 million Thai tourists visited Phuket. Phuket has also become a popular destination for yachts and cruise tourism that also visit the beautiful islands of Ranong Province. Ranong is famous for its hot springs, where various first-class hotels cater to visitors. In 2018, there were 1,025,144 visitors to Ranong, 94% of which were domestic tourists (Table 25).

Table 25: Number of Visitors to Phuket and Ranong

Item	Number of Visitors (persons)		
	2017	2018[a]	Percent Change (%)
Visitors to Phuket	14,012,863	14,383,348	2.64
Thais	3,903,481	4,054,396	3.87
Foreigners	10,109,382	10,328,952	2.17
Visitors to Ranong	977,472	1,025,144	4.88
Thais	922,649	966,915	4.80
Foreigners	54,823	58,229	6.21

[a] Preliminary.
Source: Ministry of Tourism and Sports, 2019.

Findings and Recommendations

EC5 is strategically positioned as a maritime gateway connecting to Bay of Bengal Initiative for Multi-Sectoral Technical and Economic Cooperation (BIMSTEC) and the regional tourism hub in Thailand. The overall assessment found that transport systems—roads, ports, and airports in EC5 are in good condition. However, Ranong Port is underutilized because there are no cargo transports to or from any port in BIMSTEC, and IMT-GT member countries only transport equipment to the oil rig in Andaman Sea. Phuket Deep Sea Port is designed as a pier for handling goods. Currently, more cruises have visited continuously and increasingly every year. Therefore, there is high potential to develop Phuket Port to accommodate cruise services and develop Phuket Port from the port of call to homeport.

Ranong and Phuket airports are in good condition and accommodate millions of passengers every year. However, there is no flight connection to any airport in the IMT-GT state and province.

The integration of EC5 with Phuket and Krabi will serve as the driving force to attract more tourists along the EC2 from Thailand to tourist destinations in Malaysia and Indonesia on a continuous basis.

Proposed Reconfiguration

The proposed configuration of the EC5 will include Phangnga and Krabi into the corridor. EC5 in Thailand will thus consist of Ranong, Phuket, Phangnga, and Krabi, (Maps 13 and 14) to integrate tourism activities from Krabi and Phuket to Ranong. EC5 will link with EC1 in Chumphon and Surat Thani via Highway No. 4 to enable Ranong residents to earn more income from tourism and trade.

EC5 can play the role as tourism integration corridor due to its interlink with the EC1 from Chumphon and Surat Thani or Royal Coast and Andaman Route (the Gulf of Thailand and the Andaman Sea) and the EC2 Satun, Trang, Krabi, and Phangnga, which will position the EC5 as hub and spoke for tourism (Ranong and Phangnga as spoke and Phuket and Krabi as hub). EC5 will feed tourists from EC1, EC5, to EC2 and onward to Malaysia and Indonesia along the EC2. Ranong Port can be the IMT-GT trade gateway to BIMSTEC.

**Map 13: Southwestern Thailand–Northern Sumatera–Northwestern Malaysia Economic Corridor
(Reconfigured Economic Corridor 5)**

Source: Asian Development Bank.

Map 14: Southwestern Thailand–Northern Sumatera–Northwestern Malaysia Economic Corridor (Reconfigured Economic Corridor 5) - Thailand

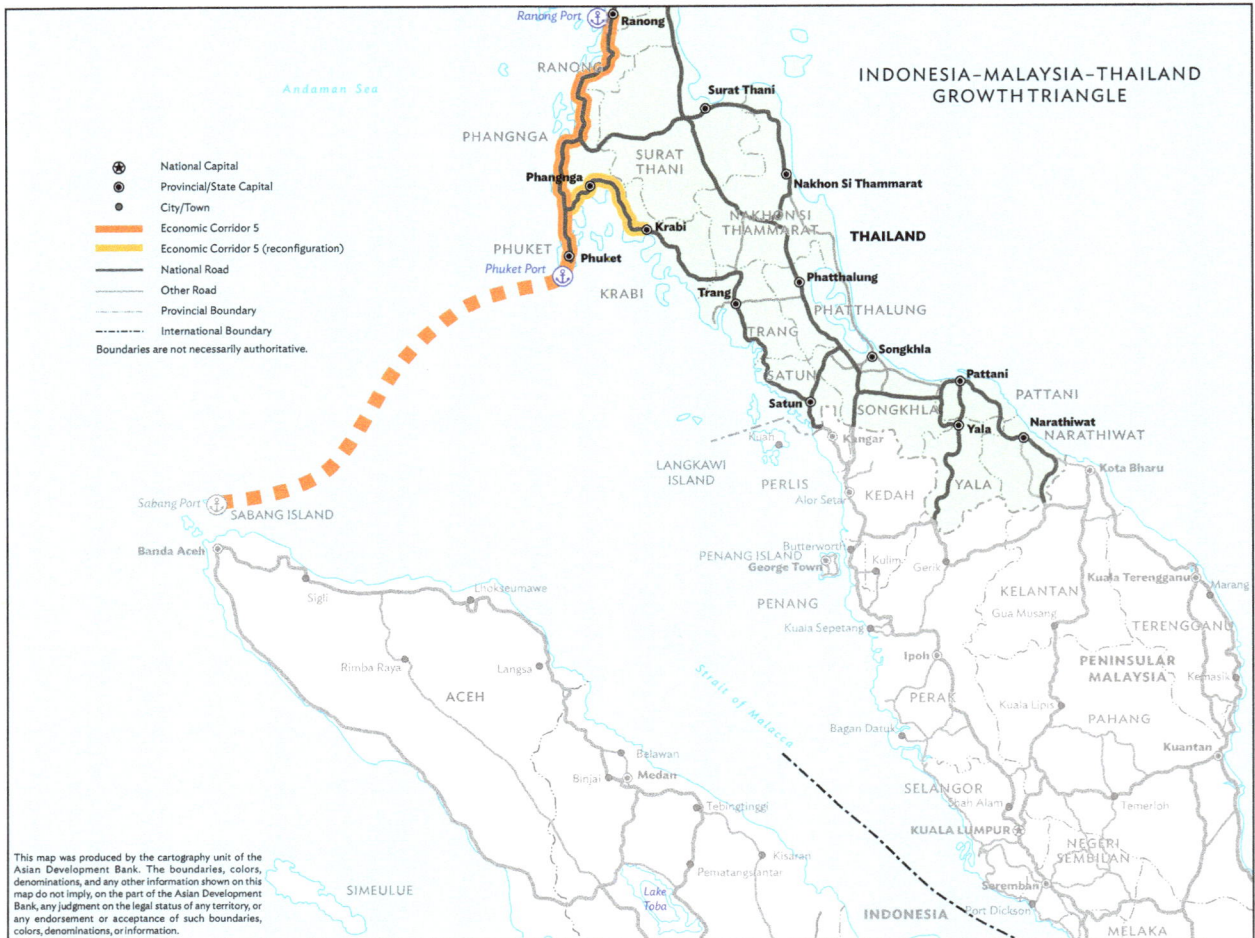

Source: Asian Development Bank.

No additional nodes are proposed in Sumatera, Indonesia. However, Malaysia has included Langkawi to be part of EC5 to enable Malaysia to tap into the tourism opportunities in the corridor. The island will serve as a new link between Sabang and Phuket to develop the Sabang–Langkawi–Phuket Tourism Development Belt. Langkawi's economy is based on tourism, which is an important source of income for the state.

Table 26 shows EC5 existing and additional provinces and nodes by type.

EC5 has been renamed Southwestern Thailand–Northern Sumatera–Northwestern Malaysia Economic Corridor.

Table 26: Economic Corridor 5: Existing and Additional Provinces and Nodes, by Type

Province/State	Node	Type			
		CAP	COM	MGP	TOUR
INDONESIA					
Aceh	Banda Aceh	✓			
	Sabang City		✓		
	Ulee Lheue Port			✓	
	Malahayati Port			✓	
	Sabang Port		✓	✓	✓
	Balohan Port			✓	
MALAYSIA					
Kedah	Langkawi*				✓
	Teluk Ewa Port*			✓	
THAILAND					
Ranong	Ranong City	✓	✓		✓
	Ranong Port			✓	
Phuket	Phuket City	✓	✓		✓
	Phuket Port			✓	
Krabi*	Krabi City*	✓	✓		✓
Phangnga*	Phangnga City*	✓			

BCP = border crossing point, CAP = capital, COM = commercial, MGP = maritime gateway port, TOUR = tourism.
Note: * denotes additional provinces and nodes.
Source: Study team.

CHAPTER

4

PROPOSED ROUTE FOR
ECONOMIC CORRIDOR 6

Overview

The sixth economic corridor (EC6) was proposed by Thailand in the 24th IMT-GT Ministerial Meeting held in Melaka on 1 October 2018. The proposed EC6 is envisaged to open new trade routes between Southern Thailand and Malaysia through the East Coast Rail Link (ECRL). The ECRL, which is part of the PRC's Belt and Road Initiative (BRI), will connect Peninsular Malaysia's east and west coasts. The proposed corridor is perceived to be a game changer for IMT-GT as it creates opportunities for expanded trade with the PRC and Europe. Malaysia is currently undertaking rapid and massive development of its eastern coast to create catalytic growth centers that could leverage on infrastructure expansion in the next 10 years. EC6 will connect the east coast of Thailand to the east coast of Malaysia. It will link Thailand's southern provinces of Pattani, Yala, and Narathiwat with the east coast to link with Malaysia at Perak and Kelantan and beyond.

An objective of the study is to recommend the route for EC6. In configuring the route, the study took into account (i) the development strategy of the countries in the areas to be traversed by the route; (ii) existing connectivity between provinces, states, and nodes along the route; and (iii) economic opportunities and potential value chain linkages.

Proposed Route

Thailand proposed to integrate the part of Extended EC1 (Pattani, Yala, and Narathiwat) as EC6, to link with the eastern part of Malaysia (Map 15). Thailand's strategy for EC6 is to integrate provincial production networks in the three provinces—Pattani, Yala, and Narathiwat—with halal and other food supply chains in Songkhla and nearby areas (EC1). Because of security issues that limit outside investments, agricultural produce from the three provinces is transported to nearby provincial factories or exported directly through the Thai–Malaysian borders. Enhancing the domestic value chain will boost the productivity and economic resiliency of provinces in Southern Thailand. The three provinces can also leverage their shared culture and history to expand opportunities for tourism.

The EC6 route will start from Pattani, continuing south to Yala and Narathiwat. Narathiwat will connect with Kelantan. In Narathiwat, there are three BCPs at the border with Kelantan: Su-ngai Kolok, Buketa, and Tak Bai. Narathiwat links with Kelantan through a bridge across the Kolok River, at Tak Bai (Narathiwat) and Tumpat (Kelantan), and a second bridge at the border of Su-ngai Kolok (Narathiwat) and Rantau Panjang (Kelantan). The rail link at Su-ngai Kolok–Rantau Panjang–Pasir Mas–Tumpat, which is currently dormant, will be reactivated. Narathiwat is connected to Kota Bharu (Kelantan) through Asian Highway No. 17 (Thailand) and No. 7 (Malaysia). There are existing overland routes from Songkhla to Penang Port and further to Port Klang, which is the end point of ECRL on the west coast.

Narathiwat is the only province that shares a border with Kelantan. There are three BCPs at the Narathiwat–Kelantan borders:

(i)   Su-ngai Kolok–Rantau Panjang,

(ii)   Ban Buketa–Bukit Bunga/Tanah Merah, and

(iii)   Tak Bai–Pengkalan Kubor.

Map 15: Southeastern Thailand–Eastern Malaysia–Southern Sumatera Economic Corridor (Proposed Route for Economic Corridor 6) - Thailand-Malaysia

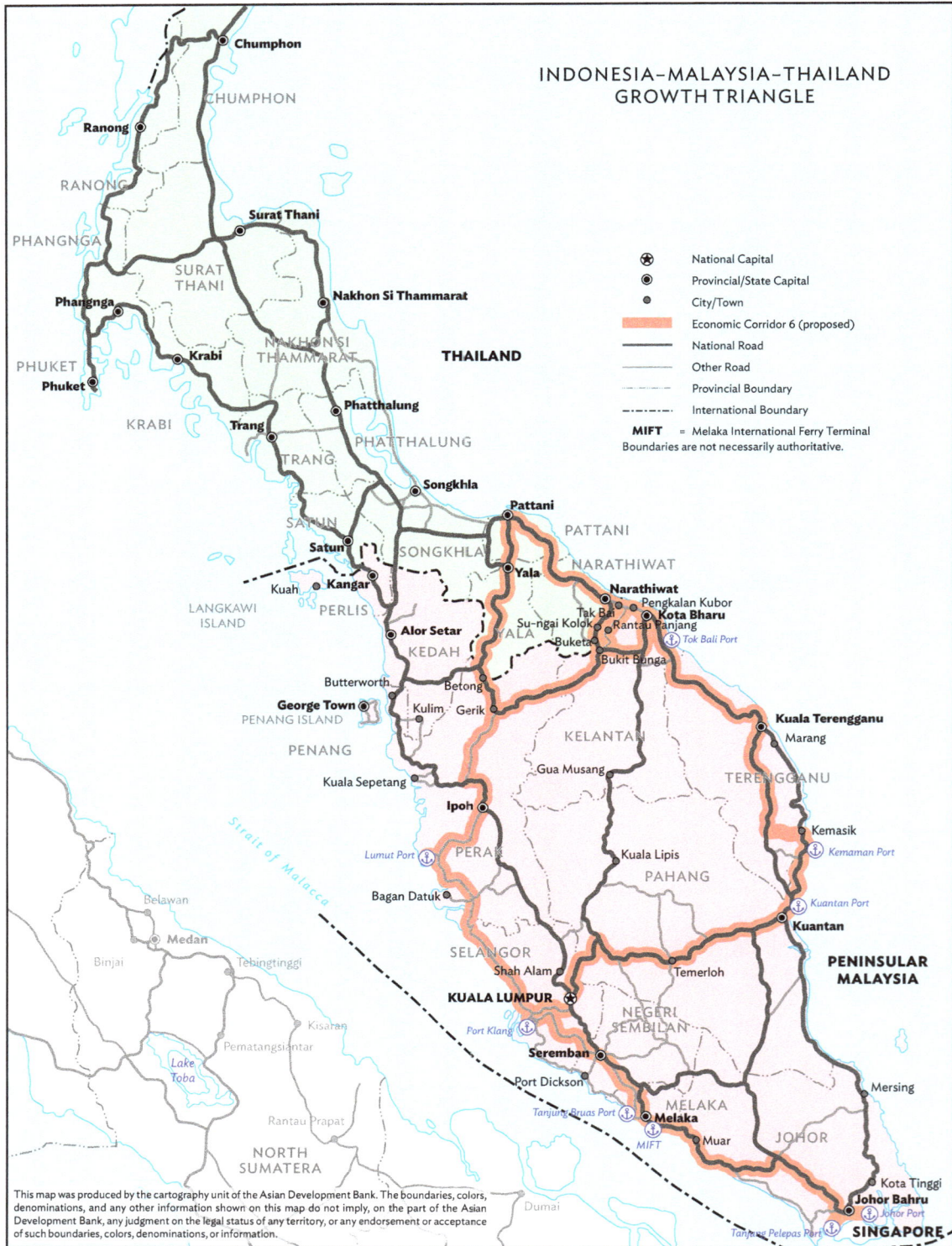

Source: Asian Development Bank.

Except for Tak Bai–Pengkalan Kubor, the links between border towns are via roads and bridges. Tak Bai and Pengkalan Kubor are separated by the Kolok River and linked via ferry service. Another entry point to Malaysia is at Betong (Yala) connecting to Pengkalan Hulu in Perak. This link is part of EC2.

Malaysia Strategy, States, and Nodes

The EC6 route in Malaysia is proposed to start from the BCPs in Kelantan (bordering Thailand) extending southward to Melaka (Tanjung Bruas Port) and Johor. Melaka will link to Dumai (Riau Province) under EC4. Johor will link with Batam (Riau Islands), which Indonesia has proposed to be part of EC6 (footnote 7).

There are two alternative routes from Kelantan to Melaka. These routes are henceforth referred to as EC6 Malaysia Route 1 (EC6-MR1), and EC6 Malaysia Route 2 (EC6-MR2).

EC6–MR1. From the BCPs in Kelantan, this route links with Kota Bahru—the start point of ECRL—and passes through Tok Bali, Kuala Terengganu, Kemaman Port, Kuantan City, Kuantan Port, up to Tanjung Bruas Port in Melaka. The total distance is 832 km from Kota Bahru to Tanjung Bruas Port in Melaka. This route has an eastward orientation.

The key maritime gateway in EC6-MR1 is Kuantan Port (Pahang). Kuantan Port is the designated port for the PRC–Malaysia BRI and plays a strategic role in expanding trade with the PRC and Europe. Kuantan Port has maritime links to Songkhla Port (Thailand), Cambodia, the Lao People's Democratic Republic (Lao PDR), and Viet Nam, and the northeast Asia region. There is no maritime connectivity between Kuantan Port (Pahang) and Sumatera Ports but has connectivity with Laem Chabang Port in Bangkok.

Two other ports along this route are Kemaman Port (Terengganu) and Tok Bali Port (Kelantan). Kemaman Port is one of the deepest seaports in Malaysia and fast-emerging as the new gateway to the Asia and Pacific region. Tok Bali Port (Kelantan) is a minor fishing port. Under the East Coast Economic Region (ECER) Blueprint 2.0 (2018–2025), this port will be expanded to serve as a feeder to Kuantan Port.

EC6–MR2. From the BCPs in Kelantan, this route links with Kota Bahru—the start point of ECRL—and passes through Perak (Gerik, Ipoh City, Lumut Port), Port Klang, and up to Tanjung Bruas Port in Melaka. The total distance is 794 km. This route has a westward orientation.

The key maritime gateways in EC6-MR2 are Lumut Port (Pahang), Port Klang (Selangor), and Tanjung Bruas Port (Melaka).

(i)   Port Klang is the end point of ECRL and is expected to significantly increase its cargo traffic volume when the rail project is completed. As Malaysia's premier port, it services routes to various international destinations. It links with other Malaysia ports along the western coast of the Peninsula, as well as with Sumatera ports across the Strait of Malacca, including Belawan (EC2), Palembang (EC3), and Dumai (EC4).

(ii)   Lumut Port is a maritime gateway to trade with Southeast Asia, India, the Middle East, the PRC, Australia, and the Atlantic Basin. There is an overland route from Songkhla Port to Lumut Port up to Port Klang.

(iii)   Tanjung Bruas Port, which is a secondary port, has trade links with ports in Sumatera, especially with Palembang and Lhokseumawe. It also has links with ports in Bangkok (Thailand), Jurong (Singapore), Kaohsiung, (Taipei,China), Saiki (Japan), and Humen (PRC).

Indonesia Strategy, States, and Nodes

Under the Rencana Pembangunan Jangka Menengah Nasional (National Medium-Term Development Plan) 2020–2024, Sumatera Island development will be directed to the downstreaming of agriculture, fisheries, and mining-based industries to create added value through processing raw materials into semi-finished and finished materials. This could be achieved by optimizing the benefits of infrastructure such as the Trans-Sumatera toll road, airports, and ports. In addition, the development of economic zones along the east coast corridor of Sumatera is expected to generate investments in downstream industries that could enhance export-oriented growth. The leading commodities identified in the National Medium-Term Development Plan 2020–2024 are cacao, coconut, palm oil, rubber, coffee, pepper, nutmeg, sugarcane, gold, tin, petroleum, natural gas, coal, capture fisheries, and aquaculture. Downstream activities in these commodities will be promoted in SEZs, industrial zones, free trade zones, and free ports.[8]

Regional development in Sumatera is carried out through two main approaches: the growth approach and the equity approach. These two approaches are reflected in the designated growth corridor and the island-based equalization and equal distribution corridor. The growth corridor is oriented toward stimulating national economic growth by accelerating the development of growth areas. The growth areas that have been identified in the plan include the national activity center, regional activity centers, SEZs, industrial zones, and national strategic tourism zones, as well as cities and urban agglomeration areas in districts and cities located in the growth corridor. The equal distribution corridor is oriented toward more equitable provision of basic services through the establishment of regional activity centers and local activity centers that can provide a wider reach in areas covered in the corridor.

The nodes in the proposed EC6 will include (Map 16):

(i)   Riau Islands: Batam and Tanjung Pinang (Bintan);

(ii)   Bangka Belitung Islands: Pangkal Pinang (Bangka) and Tanjung Pandan (Belitung);

(iii)   South Sumatera: Palembang;

(iv)   Jambi: Jambi City;

(v)   Bengkulu: Bengkulu City; and

(vi)   Lampung: Bandar Lampung.

---

[8]   S. N. I. Raharjo. 2023. *Review and Assessment of the Indonesia–Malaysia–Thailand Growth Triangle Economic Corridors: Indonesia Country Report*. Manila: Asian Development Bank.

Map 16: Southeastern Thailand–Eastern Malaysia–Southern Sumatera Economic Corridor (Proposed Route for Economic Corridor 6)

Source: Asian Development Bank.

Table 27 shows the proposed EC6 provinces, states, and nodes, by type.

Table 27: Economic Corridor 6: Proposed Provinces, States, and Nodes, by Type

Province/State	Node	Type				
		CAP	COM	BCP	MGP	TOUR
INDONESIA						
South Sumatera	Palembang	✓	✓			✓
Jambi	Jambi	✓	✓			
Lampung	Bandar Lampung	✓	✓		✓	
Bengkulu	Bengkulu	✓	✓		✓	
Riau Islands	Batam		✓		✓	
	Tanjungpinang	✓			✓	
Bangka Belitung Islands	Tanjung Pandan		✓			✓
	Pangkalpinang	✓				
MALAYSIA						
Kelantan	Rantau Panjang			✓		✓
	Bukit Bunga			✓		✓
	Pengkalan Kubor			✓		✓
	Kota Bharu	✓				
	Tok Bali Port		✓		✓	
Terengganu	Kuala Terengganu	✓				
	Kemaman Port		✓			
Pahang	Kuantan	✓	✓	✓		
	Kuantan Port		✓			
Perak	Ipoh	✓				
	Lumut Port				✓	
Selangor	Port Klang				✓	
Melaka	Melaka City	✓				
	Tanjung Bruas Port				✓	
	Melaka International Cruise Terminal				✓	
Johor	Johor Bahru	✓				
	Tanjung Pelepas Port, Gelang Patah				✓	
	Johor Port, Pasir Gudang				✓	
Negeri Sembilan	Seremban	✓				
	Port Dickson				✓	✓
THAILAND						
Pattani	Pattani City	✓				
Yala	Yala City	✓				
	Betong			✓		✓
Narathiwat	Narathiwat City	✓	✓			
	Tak Bai		✓	✓		
	Su-ngai Kolok		✓	✓		
	Buketa			✓		

BCP = border crossing point, CAP = capital, COM = commercial, MGP = maritime gateway port, TOUR = tourism.
Source: Study team.

Status of Physical Connectivity

Road Connectivity

EC6 in Thailand starts at Mueang District and ends at the Thai–Malaysian border in Yala and Narathiwat. The route is divided into six sections: (i) Pattani Mueang District–Yala Mueang District, (ii) Yala Mueang District–Betong BCP, (iii) Pattani Mueang District–Narathiwat Mueang District, (iv) Narathiwat Mueang District–Tak Bai BCP, (v) Narathiwat Mueang District–Su-ngai Kolok BCP, and (vi) Narathiwat Mueang District–Buketa BCP. Table 28 indicates the physical location and status of each route.

In summary, the route from Pattani, Yala, and Narathiwat with the east coast link to Malaysia at Perak and Kelantan covers between 38.2 km and 131 km depending on the start and end points. It has two and four traffic lanes. In all six sections, the road surface is smooth and the route is safe (equipped with traffic signs, traffic lines, complete and undamaged safety equipment, curved guideposts, and complete guardrail in good condition).

Table 28: Economic Corridor 6: Start and End Points in Thailand

Start Point	End Point	Route	Distance (km)	Traffic Lanes	Road Classification
Pattani	Yala	410	42	2–4	Class II
Yala	Betong	410	131	2–4	Class II/I
Patani	Narathiwat	42	94.8	4	Class II/I
Narathiwat	Tak Bai	4084/42/4327	38.2	2–4	Class I
Narathiwat	Su-ngai Kolok	4084/42	64.5	4	Class I
Narathiwat	Buketa	4055/4056/4193/4057	79.2	2–4	Class II/I

km = kilometer.
Source: Compiled by the author.

Rail Connectivity

The main rail route goes southeast from Hat Yai to Su-ngai Kolok on the Thai–Malaysian Border. The route from Hat Yai District to Su-ngai Kolok District covers 214 km (Map 17). There is a rail link at Su-ngai Kolok (last station on the southeast branch) across the Kolok River to Rantau Panjang (Malaysia) (Map 18), but there are no cross-border passenger train services there. There are also no cross-border bus services between Thailand and Malaysia on the southeast coast of the Thai–Malaysian border.

Map 17: Rail Routes in Thailand

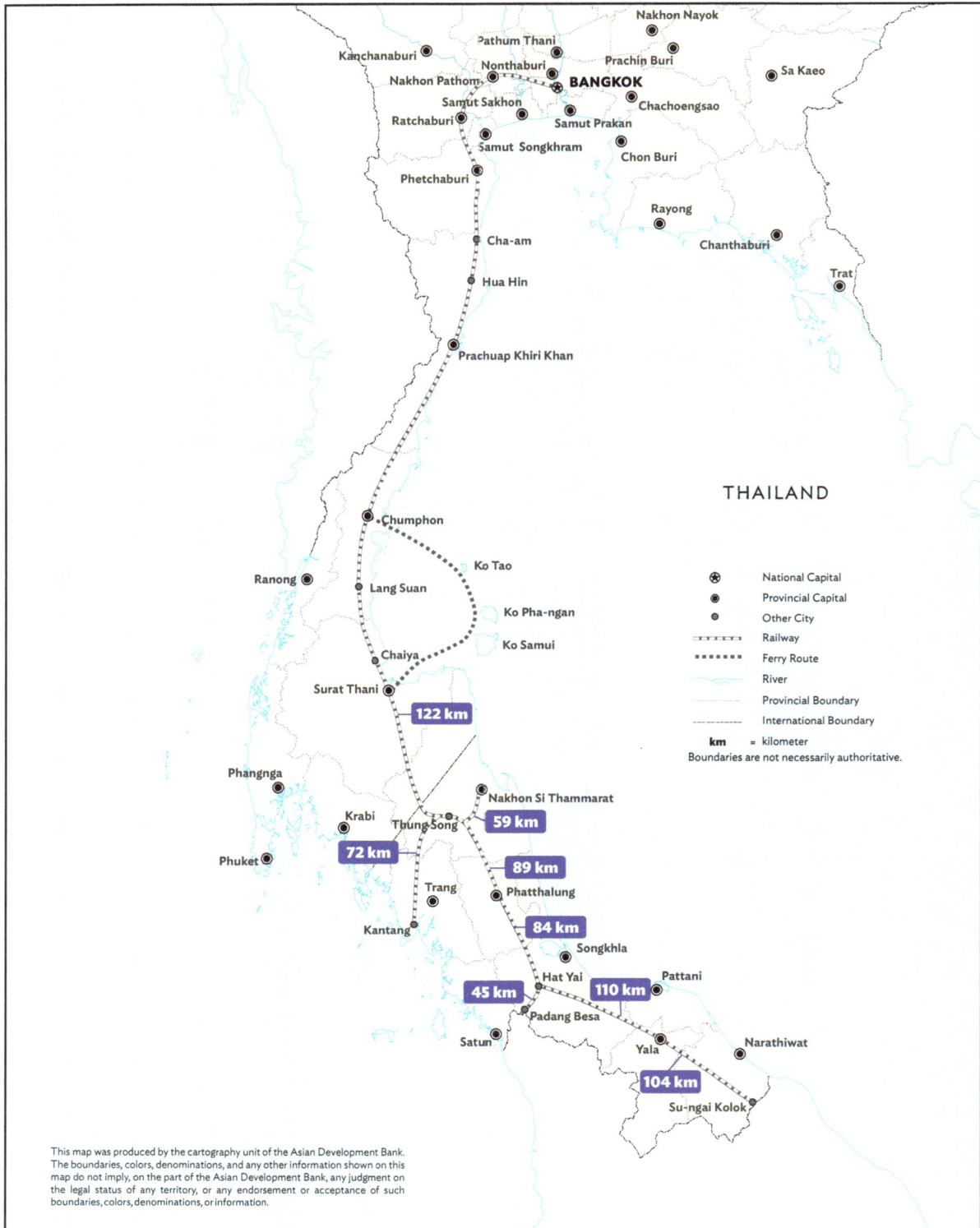

Source: Asian Development Bank.

Map 18: Rail Routes in Malaysia

Legend
⊛ National Capital
⊙ Provincial/State Capital
SRT Southern Line
KTMB West Coast Line
KTMB East Coast Line
KTMB Kargo Line
National Road
Other Road
Provincial Boundary
International Boundary

Boundaries are not necessarily authoritative.

State Railway of Thailand (SRT)
• Southern Line: Bangkok–Hat Yai–Padang Besar/Su-ngai Kolok

Keretapi Tanah Melayu Berhad (KTMB)/ Malayan Railways Limited
• West Coast Line
  • North Line: Padang Besar–Tanjong Malim
  • Central Line: Tanjong Malim–Kuala Lumpur
  • South Line: Seremban–Woodlands
• East Coast Line: Tumpat–Gemas
• Kargo Line: Kuala Lumpur–Port Klang

This map was produced by the cartography unit of the Asian Development Bank. The boundaries, colors, denominations, and any other information shown on this map do not imply, on the part of the Asian Development Bank, any judgment on the legal status of any territory, or any endorsement or acceptance of such boundaries, colors, denominations, or information.

Source: Asian Development Bank.

When the railway connection from Su-ngai Kolok Railway Station to Pasir Mas Railway Station in Kelantan (covering 18 km in Thailand and 2 km in Malaysia) will be finished, it will be possible for Thailand to connect to the ECRL. The ECRL links the route between Kuantan Port; Pahang; and Klang Port, Selangor, with Malaysia's route on the east coast from Kelantan–Terengganu–Pahang–Selangor. This land bridge connecting Malaysia's east and west coast without having to go through the Strait of Malacca will transform the current trade route in the region. Kuantan Port is the designated port in Malaysia for the PRC's BRI. EC6 can be connected with the PRC and European trade routes via Kuantan Port and Port Klang. The entire route of ECRL covers 620 km and the land bridge in Malaysia covers 250 km.

Cross-Border Nodes

Cross-border nodes on the EC6 route consist of four BCPs in Betong, Tak Bai, Su-ngai Kolok, and Buketa (Table 29).

Table 29: Distance Between Cross-Border Nodes

Start Point	End Point	Route	Distance (km)	Traffic Lanes	Road Classification	Road Condition
Tak Bai BCP	Su-ngai Kolok BCP	42	39	4	Class I	Good
Su-ngai Kolok BCP	Buketa BCP	4057	31	2–4	Class I	Good
Buketa BCP	Betong BCP	4057/4193, /4115/524 4271/ 4273/ 410	216	2–4	Class I	Good

BCP = border crossing point, km = kilometer.
Note: The route is not widely used as it passes the mountainous region. Traveling takes quite a long time with approximately 4.5 hours.
Source: Compiled by the author.

Maritime Connectivity

There are no major maritime routes for Thailand in EC6. The ports along the coast of Narathiwat and Pattani are used mainly as fisherfolks' pier. There is no commercial port for transport of goods and passengers.

Air Links

Thailand airports located in EC6 are Narathiwat Airport and Betong Airport (Yala). Narathiwat Airport is situated at Ban Thon, Kok Kian Subdistrict, Mueang District, Narathiwat and is under the supervision of the Department of Airports, Ministry of Transport. Narathiwat Airport services mainly domestic flights by Thai Smile Airways and Thai AirAsia, except for international flights by Thai Airways to Mecca during Hajj (Table 30).

Table 30: Flight Routes at Narathiwat Airport

Airlines	Destinations	Types of Flights
Thai Smile Airways	Bangkok via Suvarnabhumi	Domestic
Thai AirAsia	Bangkok via Don Mueang	Domestic
Thai Airways	Only during the period of the Hajj: Medina (outgoing), Jeddah (incoming)	International

Source: Compiled by the author.

Betong Airport is situated at Yarom Subdistrict, Betong District, Yala (12 km from Betong). It is under the supervision of the Department of Airports. The Betong Airport was expected to open in January 2022 and it is expected to help alleviate the difficulty of land travel in Yala's mountainous terrain and support tourism.

Trade

The growth rate of the Thai–Malaysian border trade in Pattani during 2014–2018 was 291.5%, with increase in exports by 286.5%, while import value decreased by 312.5% (Table 31). The export products via Pattani Customs House were mainly commodities products (Table 32). The highest export value was rice valued at $3.3 million followed by shallots, corn seeds, and sacks. The only import product via Pattani Customs House was peeled coconuts.[9]

Table 31: Export–Import Value at Pattani Customs House

Customs Houses	Trade Value ($ million)					
	2014	2015	2016	2017	2018	CAGR (%)
Pattani Customs House						
Export	0.014	0.00	0.0	3.6	3.10	286.5
Import	0.003	0.08	1.0	4.1	0.87	(312.6)
Total	**0.017**	**0.08**	**1.0**	**7.7**	**3.90**	**291.5**

( ) = negative, CAGR = compound annual growth rate.
Source: Department of Foreign Trade. 2019; Bank of Thailand. https://www.bot.or.th/App/BTWS_STAT/statistics/ReportPage.aspx?reportID=123&language=th (accessed 26 February 2020).

Table 32: Pattani Customs House: Top Export-Import Values in 2018

Rank	Export	Weight (kg)	Value ($ million)	Import[a]	Weight (kg)	Value ($ million)
1	Rice (white rice 5%)	8,514,000	3.300	Peeled coconuts	4,045,000	1.1
2	Shallots	150,000	0.074			
3	Corn seeds	230,000	0.064			
4	Sacks	44,000	0.002			

kg = kilogram.
[a] Import data at Pattani are not available.
Source: Pattani Customs House. 2019; Bank of Thailand. https://www.bot.or.th/App/BTWS_STAT/statistics/ReportPage.aspx?reportID=123&language=th (accessed 26 February 2020).

9   Only peeled coconuts have been record in 2018.

The growth rates of the Thai–Malaysian border trade in Betong during 2014–2018 was at 0.53%, with an increase in export valued at 0.92%, while import value decreased by 7.95% (Table 33). In 2018, the export via Betong Customs House were rubber products, finished rubber, fresh fruits, plywood, clothes, automotive assembly parts, cracker and wafer, processed para wood and sports shoes. Products trade in Betong crossing point mainly commercial products which export as transshipment products to Port Klang and Malaysia market.

The import products were liquid ammonia; Styrene Butadiene rubber; lubricants used for rubber industry; formalin; used centrifuge for concentrated latex; herbal capsule; used rubber grinder; rubber grinder (repair); used equipment to press, cut, peel, saw, and cure rubber; processed wood; and melamine used in plywood industry. Import products via Betong crossing point were also commercial products used for rubber and wood processing industries in Thailand (Table 34).

Table 33: Export–Import Value at Thai–Malaysian Border in Betong

Province	Trade value ($ million)					CAGR (%)
	2014	2015	2016	2017	2018	
Yala	108.8	77.1	78.8	122.9	111.1	0.53
Export	103.3	74.0	75.8	119.4	107.2	0.92
Import	5.5	3.1	3.0	3.5	3.9	(7.95)

( ) = negative, CAGR = compound annual growth rate.
Source: Department of Foreign Trade. 2019; Bank of Thailand. https://www.bot.or.th/App/BTWS_STAT/statistics/ReportPage.aspx?reportID=123&language=th (accessed 26 February 2020).

Table 34: Betong Customs House: Top 10 Export–Import Values in 2018

Rank	Export	Weight (kg)	Value ($ million)	Import	Weight (kg)	Value ($ million)
1	Rubber products	75,587,803	83.6	Liquid ammonia	2,433,000	1.1
2	Finished rubber (rubber mixed with chemicals)	16,413,960	25.1	Styrene Butadiene rubber	295,680	.66
3	Durians, langsats, rambutans, rose apples, cempedaks	8,345,076	6.4	Other lubricants used for rubber industry	246,080	.22
4	Plywood	2,707,200	1.1	Formalin	375,000	.15
5	Mangoes, mangosteens, guavas	1,304,527	.06	Used centrifuge for concentrated latex	39,963	.13
6	Clothes and items accompanying children's clothes	15,647	.43	Herbal capsule	3,220	.12
7	Automotive assembly parts	17,827	408	Used rubber grinder, rubber grinder (repair)	28,548	.11
8	Cracker, wafer	96,370	295	Used equipment to press, cut, peel, saw, and cure rubber	29,090	.10
9	Processed para wood	578,425	223	Processed wood	124,003	.09
10	Sports shoes with PV rubber sole	6,656	205	Melamine used in plywood industry	66,000	.09

kg = kilogram.
Source: Betong Customs House. 2019; Bank of Thailand. https://www.bot.or.th/App/BTWS_STAT/statistics/ReportPage.aspx?reportID=123&language=th (accessed 26 February 2020).

The growth rate of the Thai–Malaysian border trade in Tak Bai, Narathiwat during 2014–2018 was at 4.51%, with increase in export value at 0.08%, while import value decreased at 6.63% (Table 35).

In 2018, the exports via Tak Bai Customs House were cigarettes, tapioca flour, granite, frozen Siamese glassfish, frozen white leg shrimps, frozen mackerel scads, frozen bigeye scads, frozen Sardinellas, frozen hardtail scads, and shoes (used).

The imports were peeled coconuts, frozen yellow-stripe scads, frozen squids, frozen lizardfish, frozen white knife fish, frozen Bonito Tunas, frozen yellow goatfish, frozen threadfin bream fish, frozen bass, and used clothes and automotive assembly parts. Import and export products in Tak Bai, Narathiwat were mainly frozen seafood, reflecting that there were seafood supply chain industries between Pattani, Narathiwat and Malaysia. (Table 36).

Table 35: Export–Import Value at Thai–Malaysian Border in Tak Bai, Narathiwat

Province	Trade value ($ million)					CAGR (%)
	2014	2015	2016	2017	2018	
Narathiwat	95.6	94.8	135.3	128.5	114.1	4.51
Export	32.9	32.9	40.9	33.9	33.0	0.08
Import	62.7	61.9	94.4	94.6	81.1	(6.63)

( ) = negative, CAGR = compound annual growth rate.
Source: Department of Foreign Trade. 2019; Bank of Thailand. https://www.bot.or.th/App/BTWS_STAT/statistics/ReportPage.aspx?reportID=123&language=th (accessed 26 February 2020).

Table 36: Tak Bai Customs House: Top 10 Export–Import Values in 2018

Rank	Export	Weight (kg)	Value ($ million)	Import	Weight (kg)	Value ($ million)
1	Cigarettes	694,496	6.7	Peeled coconuts	34,991,000	9.5
2	Tapioca flour	7,472,600	3.1	Frozen yellow-stripe scads	523,320	.33
3	Granite	349,000,000	2.6	Frozen squids	195,100	.20
4	Frozen Siamese glassfish	780,180	.48	Frozen lizardfish	265,900	.20
5	Frozen white leg shrimps	156,180	.48	Frozen white knifefish	208,900	.15
6	Frozen mackerel scads	571,380	.44	Frozen Bonito Tunas	151,800	.11
7	Frozen bigeye scads	276,000	.43	Frozen yellow goatfish	161,450	.11
8	Frozen Sardinellas	345,180	.43	Frozen threadfin bream fish	139,710	.01
9	Frozen hardtail scads in whole	449,070	.42	Frozen bass in whole	151,850	.01
10	Other shoes (used)	1,050,750	.36	Used clothes and other used items	172,325	.01

kg = kilogram.
Source: Tak Bai Customs House. 2019; Bank of Thailand. https://www.bot.or.th/App/BTWS_STAT/statistics/ReportPage.aspx?reportID=123&language=th (accessed 26 February 2020).

Buketa Customs House had the total trade value of $0.29 million, or decreased 47.9%, with export valued $0.28 million, or decreased 47.8%, while import valued $0.01 million, or increased 42.2%. Thailand had trade surplus of $0.27 million.

Table 37: Export–Import Value at Customs Houses in Su-ngai Kolok and Buketa

Customs Houses	Trade Value ($ million)					
	2014	2015	2016	2017	2018	CAGR (%)
Su-ngai Kolok Customs House	89.0	2.6	90.1	93.7	89.8	0.22
Export	24.4	.71	15.2	13.8	13.6	(13.6)
Import	64.6	1.9	74.9	79.9	76.2	4.2
Buketa Customs House	...	...	1.0	.71	.29	(47.9)
Export	...	...	1.0	.70	.28	(47.8)
Import	...	...	.03	.01	.01	(42.2)
Total	89.0	2.6	91.1	94.4	90.0	0.22

... = not available, () = negative, CAGR = compound annual growth rate.
Source: Department of Foreign Trade, 2019; Bank of Thailand. https://www.bot.or.th/App/BTWS_STAT/statistics/ReportPage.aspx?reportID=123&language=th.

The growth rate of the Thai–Malaysian border trade in Su-ngai Kolok during 2014–2018 was at 0.22%, with decrease in export value at 13.6%, while import value increase at 4.2% (Table 37).

In 2018, the export via Su-ngai Kolok Customs House were frozen short mackerel, cup lump, tapioca flour, fabric woven, colored Roman tiles, live cattle, pumping machine, mixed rice flour, glutinous rice flour, instant noodles, and fresh mangoes.

The import via Su-ngai Kolok Customs House were processed wood, frozen longtail tunas, asphalt, peeled coconuts, bread, wood scrap, salted cattle skin, wheat flour, frozen cuttlefish, and paper scrap (Table 38).

Table 38: Su-ngai Kolok Customs: House Top 10 Export–Import Values in 2018

Rank	Export	Weight (kg)	Value ($ million)	Import	Weight (kg)	Value ($ million)
1	Frozen short mackerel in whole	3,425,200	3.6	Processed wood	146,995.1	56.3
2	Cup lump	2,209,000	2.1	Frozen longtail tunas in whole	14,595.4	12.6
3	Finished tapioca flour	2,830,376	1.2	Asphalt	3,653.5	1.4
4	Fabric woven with synthetic fiber	143,364	1.1	Peeled coconuts	4,170.0	1.9
5	Colored Roman tiles made from cellulose fiber cement	4,130,384	1.0	Bread	232.7	.60
6	Live cattle	369,530	.65	Wood scrap	24,159.7	.60
7	Pumping machine	56,872	.45	Salted cattle skin in whole	916.0	.54
8	Mixed rice flour, glutinous rice flour	548,500	.44	Wheat flour	1,400.2	.53
9	Semi-instant noodles	240,648	.37	Frozen cuttlefish in whole	307.8	.29
10	Fresh mangoes	788,282	.31	Paper scrap	1,017.5	.26

kg = kilogram.
Source: Su-ngai Kolok Customs House. 2019; Bank of Thailand. https://www.bot.or.th/App/BTWS_STAT/statistics/ReportPage.aspx?reportID=123&language=th (accessed 26 February 2020).

The Thai–Malaysian border trade in Buketa Customs House during 2016–2018 had a decreasing rate at 47.9%, and decreasing export value at 47.8%. Import value also decreased at 42.3%.

Imports via the Buketa Customs House with the highest value were office or school products, engines, wooden furniture, porcelain kitchenware, and products for festivities. The export products were frozen chicken, natural rubber, coagulated rubber, bed or tablecloth, and fresh vegetables (Table 39).

Table 39: Buketa Customs House: Top Five Export–Import Values in 2018

Rank	Export	Weight (kg)	Value ($ million)	Import	Weight (kg)	Value ($ million)
1	Frozen chicken	114,204	.14	Office or school products	27,800	2
2	Natural rubber	165,000	.08	Engines	180	.89
3	Coagulated rubber	27,000	.02	Wooden furniture	7,400	.58
4	Bed or tablecloth	9,555	.02	Porcelain kitchenware	15,500	.54
5	Fresh vegetables	5,955	.01	Products for festivities	10,000	.52

kg = kilogram.
Source: Buketa Customs House. 2019; Bank of Thailand. https://www.bot.or.th/App/BTWS_STAT/statistics/ReportPage.aspx?reportID=123&language=th (accessed 26 February 2020).

Tourism

Malaysian tourists often visit Betong, Su-ngai Kolok, and Tak Bai to enjoy Thai and Chinese food during Malaysian holidays and Thai festivals. In 2018, 1.7 million tourists visited the three provinces, or 4.5% over the previous year. Yala and Narathiwat each recorded more than 680,000 visitors that year, compared to 290,000 for Pattani. Visitors to Pattani were mostly domestic tourists (99%); while in the case of Yala and Narathiwat, foreign visitors significantly outnumbered local visitors (Table 40).

Table 40: Number of Visitors to Pattani, Yala, and Narathiwat, 2017 and 2018

Item	Number of Visitors (persons)		Percent Increase (%)
	2017	2018[a]	
Pattani	**272,739**	**289,113**	**6.0**
Thais	270,575	286,621	5.9
Foreigners	2,164	2,492	15.2
Yala	**657,317**	**683,576**	**4.0**
Thais	141,012	148,451	5.3
Foreigners	516,305	535,125	3.7
Narathiwat	**665,710**	**688,448**	**3.4**
Thais	253,482	271,440	7.1
Foreigners	412,228	417,008	1.2

[a] Preliminary.
Source: Ministry of Tourism and Sports, 2019.

Industrial Activities

The Narathiwat SEZ[10] has three BCPs connecting with Malaysia: Su-ngai Kolok, Tak Bai, and Buketa, that can accommodate cross-border trade and tourism between Thailand and Malaysia. Narathiwat Airport provides transport and traveling services to both Thai and Malaysian tourists and investors. Moreover, the raw materials supporting agro-processing industries include rubber, palm oil, including cultural strengths that can efficiently develop the halal industry.

According to the information on registered enterprises in 2019, there were 364 registered enterprises with registered capital of B2,564.10 ($82.7million). The investment in the SEZ (Su-ngai Kolok subdistrict, Kok Kian subdistrict, Chehe subdistrict, La Han subdistrict, and Loh Jood subdistrict) constitutes 26.19% of investments outside the SEZ. The investment value in the SEZ constitutes 36.26% of investments outside the SEZ. Most businesses in the SEZ are SMEs constituting 99.73% with main retail or wholesale businesses such as general construction, wholesale of wood and primary processed wood products, and retail shops of other construction materials.

Recommendations

The proposed route for EC6 seeks to achieve economic and social development of the three countries. Thailand continues to attach great importance to developing the required infrastructure to strengthen its connectivity with Malaysia and Indonesia through the development of economic corridors. For EC6 in Thailand, priority will be given to the following initiatives:

(i)   utilizing multimodal connectivity covering roads, rails, seaports, airports, CIQ facilities, SEZs, ICDs, and relevant logistics facilities;

(ii)   constructing the new bridge link across Kolok River at Tak Bai, Narathiwat (Thailand)–Pengkalan Kubor, Kelantan (Malaysia);

(iii)   constructing the second bridge across Kolok River at Su-ngai Kolok–Rantau Panjang;

(iv)   upgrading the Thailand–Malaysia Friendship bridge across Kolok River at Buketa–Bukit Bunga;

(v)   connecting the railway route from Su-ngai Kolok Railway Station to Pasir Mas Railway Station in Kelantan over a distance of 20 km (2 km in Thailand and 18 km in Malaysia);

(vi)   integrate provincial production networks in EC6 with networks in EC especially for rubber latex, rubber wood, seafood, and halal food value chains; and

(vii)   promote routes for ecotourism, history, and culture among the three E6 provinces with potential to link with tourism routes in EC1 and EC5.

EC6 will be named as the **Southeastern Thailand–Eastern Malaysia–Southern Sumatera Corridor**.

---

[10]   The Narathiwat SEZs are located in five subdistricts (in five districts) with total development area of 235.17 km² along the Thailand–Malay border. These are (i) Muang Narathiwat District including Kok Kian subdistrict, (ii) Tak Bai District including Jeh Hay subdistrict, (iii) Yee Ngor District including La Harn subdistrict, (iv) Wang District including Loh Jood subdistrict, and (v) Su-ngai Kolok District including Su-ngai Kolok subdistrict.

CHAPTER

5

THE NETWORK OF IMT-GT ECONOMIC CORRIDORS

Revisiting the Economic Corridor Concept

The concept of economic corridor. Economic corridors are developed along a major transport route to provide production units with access to markets though distribution centers and gateway ports. A transport corridor is the foundation for developing an economic corridor. As the corridor develops, the "narrow" transport corridor expands as urban infrastructure, industrial parks, and other agglomeration spaces emerge as part of development plans.[11]

Economic corridor development in IMT-GT traverses national borders and as such, requires collaboration between countries to ensure that goods and peoples move seamlessly across national boundaries. These require measures such as transport and trade facilitation, to transform national corridors that are merely juxtaposed at the borders into fully functioning cross-border economic corridors. Deliberate and collaborative planning between countries is critical to optimize spatial use by taking advantage of new production, growth and logistics centers, expanded connectivity, and access to gateways. As discussed in the economic corridor chapters of this study, this approach to economic corridor development has not fully materialized in IMT-GT. For the most part, Indonesia, Malaysia, and Thailand have been pursuing strategies, programs, and projects in their respective "country segments" of the IMT-GT economic corridors rather than through a collaborative and deliberate subregional planning.

Corridor nodes. As part of the review, the study identified specific nodes in each corridor. For a given corridor, the relationship and continuity between the different nodes is important to help delineate core areas, i.e., the growth and catalytic centers from which spillovers are expected to radiate (peripheral areas). The nodes identified were the points or areas that perform catalytic roles in the corridor influence areas, with the potential to contribute to trade and economic growth by leveraging on infrastructure connectivity.

The nodes identified in this study were classified as follows:

(i)   **Capital city**: the main urban and administrative center in a province or state; the area is compact, transit-oriented, and densely populated, and where high concentrations of residential, employment, retail, and key services are located;

(ii) **Border crossing point (BCP)**: the point where border areas between two countries in the corridor converge and where customs, immigration, and quarantine (CIQ) facilities are provided to enable the entry and exit of goods across the borders;

(iii) **Commercial node**: an area where there is a high concentration of economic activity such as industrial parks, SEZs, distribution centers; usually accompanied by redevelopment around the area that includes residential, retail, and services facilities;

(iv) **Maritime gateway port**: an area for the transport of cargo and passengers to external markets and/or destinations comprising a land domain (the port's region and its locality) and the maritime domain which services ships for global trade; and

(v)   **Tourism node**: an area with a medium to high density of tourists having the full range of facilities, services, and amenities, usually part of a cluster of destinations where tourists can engage in a variety of activities beyond visiting a single attraction or tourist site.

---

[11]   C. Guina. 2023. *Review and Assessment of the Indonesia–Malaysia–Thailand Growth Triangle Economic Corridors: Integrative Report*. Manila: Asian Development Bank. The contents of this section were based on the integrative report for this study, which is published as a separate publication.

Interlink corridors. The new provinces and nodes proposed under the reconfigured corridors in Chapter 3 expanded the existing corridors significantly, resulting in interlink corridors. An interlink corridor is the "route that connects two or more points in different corridors." Interlink corridors enable corridors to function as a network, rather than as single corridors. Corridors functioning as network can change the pattern of mobility for both goods and people. They can facilitate access to a larger and more diverse base of inputs (raw materials, parts, energy, or labor) and broader markets for diverse outputs (intermediate and finished goods).

The concept of economic corridors as networks rather than as point-to-point connections implies that spatial development would need to be more deliberate and coordinated. At present, economic corridor projects are typically national projects located in a corridor; and the mere collation of these projects would be considered as the set of projects for the corridor. In a network perspective, this piecemeal approach may have to give way to a more comprehensive spatial planning aimed at reducing economic distance and overcoming trade barriers in the corridors to promote complementarities in production and trade and realize scale economies for enhanced competitiveness.

IMT-GT corridors in Thailand, namely EC1, EC2, EC5, and EC6 comprise major economic activities such as trade, investment, and tourism that can be linked across corridors. Determining interlink corridors can lead to initiatives for developing synergies in various sectors across corridors (Map 19).

(i)   **Interlink Corridor A**. The Chumphon–Ranong (EC1 and EC5) interlink corridor can facilitate transport connectivity AH2 from the central region via Highway No. 4 to Ranong Port. Ranong Port is a maritime gateway to Andaman Sea ports. Connecting EC1 and EC5 via Interlink Corridor A has the potential to increase in trade in Ranong Port, as well as tourism flows between the Gulf of Thailand and Andaman Sea downward to EC2.

(ii)   **Interlink Corridor B**. The Surat Thani–Phuket interlink corridor via Highway No. 44 can link tourism destinations in Surat Thani in EC1 along the Gulf of Thailand with tourist destinations in Phuket and Krabi in EC5. This interlink will further promote tourism between the Gulf of Thailand and the Andaman Sea to become leading tourist destinations.

(iii)   **Interlink Corridor C**. This interlink corridor links Kantang Port in Trang (EC2) with Thong Song CDC in Nakhon Si Thammarat (EC1) via rail or road systems. This interlink will increase efficiency in the transport of goods to Penang Port and attract more trade and investments along the corridors.

(iv)   **Interlink Corridor D**. This interlink corridor involves Songkhla in EC1 and Trang in EC2 with potential for enhanced trade and tourism activities between the Gulf of Thailand and the Andaman Sea. Interlink corridor D will also support Trang and Langkawi to become major gateways for trade and tourism along the corridor.

Overlapping areas. The reconfiguration of existing economic corridors has also resulted in some areas overlapping in two corridors—which present opportunities for further integration of economic activities. These overlapping corridors and the economic activities that can be synergized include the following:

(i)   EC1 and EC6 via Highway No. 406, linking rubber plantations (Surat Thani, Nakhon Si Thammarat, and Songkhla) and facilities for processed rubber (Songkhla) as well as livestock production areas (Phatthalung) with halal food industries (Pattani, Yala, and Narathiwat). The routes in these two corridors also connect production bases in industrial estates and SEZs in Songkhla and Narathiwat to trade gateways along the Thai–Malaysian border at Padang Besar, Sadao, Ban Prakop, Betong, Buketa, Su-ngai Kolok, and Tak Bai, and to Songkhla Port.

(ii)   EC5 (Phangnga and Krabi) and EC2 (Tarutao Islands, Satun) via Highway No. 4 can further connect with Langkawi and Penang in Malaysia through Tammalang Port to further develop tourism activities among the three countries. The integration of Krabi (EC2) with Phuket (EC5) will drive the attraction of more tourists along EC2 that can spill over to destinations in Malaysia and Indonesia and vice versa.

Map 19: Interlink Corridors in Thailand

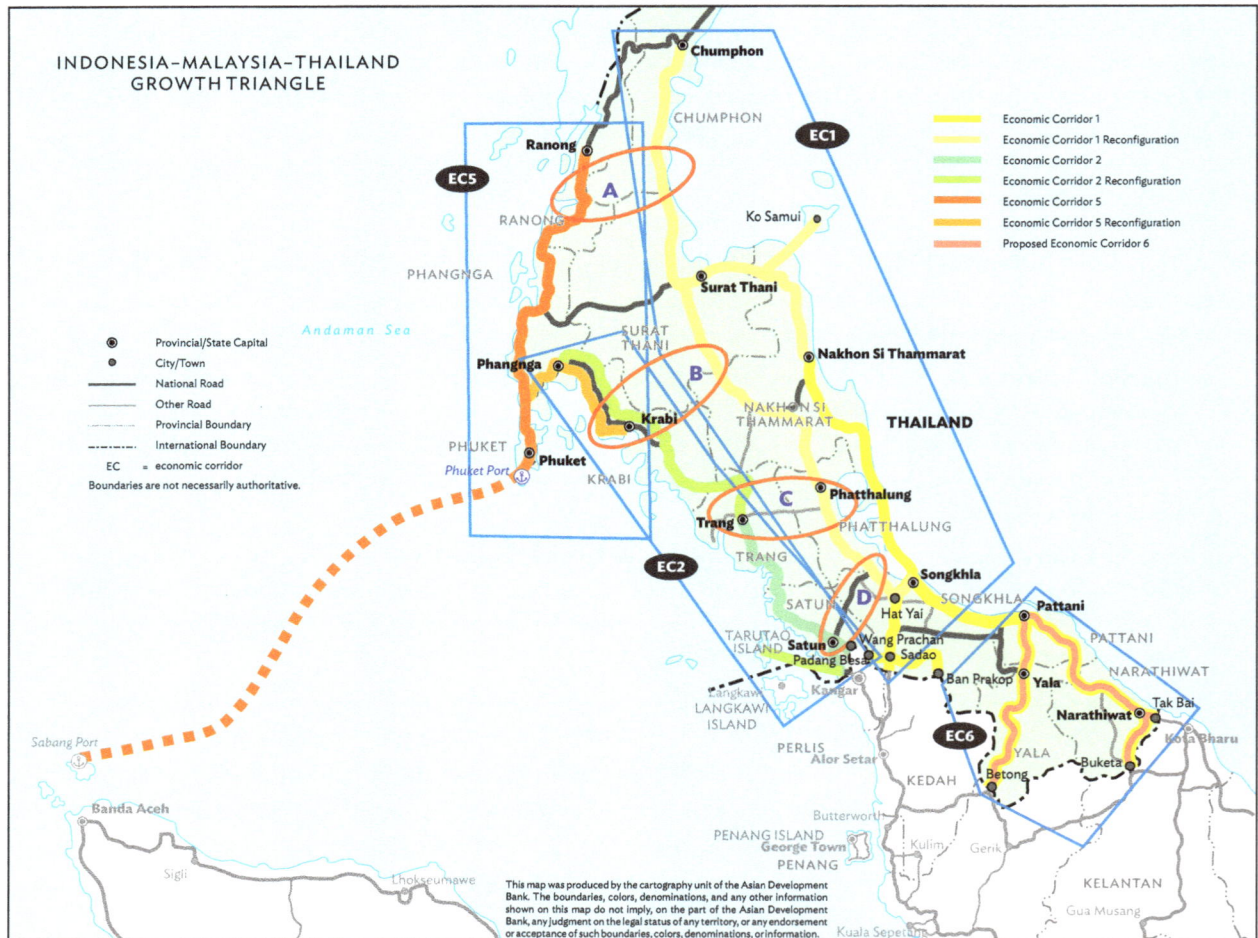

Source: Asian Development Bank.

ECONOMIC CORRIDORS FROM A VALUE CHAIN PERSPECTIVE

Economic Corridors and Value Chains

The development of value chain linkages is a key motivation for economic corridor development. This chapter looks at the value chain of three major products in IMT-GT—palm oil, rubber, and halal foods—to get a broad perspective on the geography of their production, processing, and distribution components. Value chains can be facilitated by efficient physical infrastructure to facilitate movement of goods between its various stages. Value chains can also be impacted by the location of SEZs and industrial clusters, which are crucial for attracting investments, and creating the density required to enable logistics services to operate efficiently.

The study examined the value chain of three products of strategic importance to the IMT-GT countries: palm oil, rubber, and halal food.[12] The study looked at the spatial dimensions of the different stages of these value chains focusing on the role of economic corridors.

Rubber and palm oil are major agricultural products in the southern provinces of Chumphon, Nakhon Si Thammarat, Phatthalung, Surat Thani, Songkhla, Pattani, Yala, Narathiwat, (EC1 and EC6) Ranong, Phuket (EC5) and Krabi, Trang, and Phangnga (EC2) (Tables 41 and 42). Rubber and palm oil production in Southern Thailand comprise 90% and 70%, respectively, of Thailand's total production. The government has also approved the development of Southern Thailand as an economic center for tourism and rubber and palm oil production to link with the subregion and other parts of the world.[13]

Table 41: Major Agricultural Products in Southern Thailand
(million tons)

	2018	2019	Percent Change
Palm	13.7	15.0	8.3
Rubber	2.5	2.5	(0.2)
Durian	0.254	0.421	65.6
Mangosteen	0.095	0.154	61.5

( ) = negative.
Source: Office of Agricultural Economics, Ministry of Agriculture. 2021. https://www.opsmoac.go.th/suratthani-dwl-files-421091791173.

The halal food industry is also of strategic importance to Thailand because of the large Muslim population in its southern region, and in neighboring Indonesia and Malaysia. Halal products and services have a big market in Asia, the Middle East, Europe, and Africa. In 2021, the global market value of halal products amounted to approximately $1,978 billion and is expected to reach 3,909.70 billion by 2027 with the compound annual growth rate of 11.24% during 2022–2027.[14]

About 80% of the population in the southernmost provinces of Pattani, Yala, and Narathiwat (EC6) are Muslims. This presents a sizable market for local enterprises to produce, establish, and strengthen the domestic halal products value chain. Moreover, promoting the development of the halal value chain with Indonesia and Malaysia will create an opportunity for mutual cooperation in ensuring the production of halal

---

[12]   Unlike Malaysia, the Government of Indonesia (BPS-Statistics Indonesia) does not publish halal statistics. Therefore, this report takes halal food products that are main trade commodities in Sumatera's IMT-GT area.

[13]   Developing southern Thailand as a tourism, rubber, and palm oil hub, Foreign Office, The Government Public Relations Department, Office of the Prime Minister, 2018.

[14]   IMAR. n.d. Halal Food Market: Global Industry Trends, Share, Size, Growth, Opportunity and Forecast 2022–2027. https://www.imarcgroup.com/halal-food-market.

products of the highest quality. The Southern Border Provinces Administrative Center (SBPAC), the Ministry of Agriculture and Cooperatives, and the National Food Institute are actively participating in the IMT-GT working group on halal products and services.

Palm Oil

Thailand is the third-largest palm oil producer, but it accounts for only 3.9% of the global production after Indonesia and Malaysia. In Thailand, 90.3% of palm oil plantations and their processing facilities are in the south, with the provinces of Krabi, Surat Thani, and Chumphon, producing 65% of the country's palm oil plantations. The remaining 9.97% of palm oil plantations is found in the center, north, and northeast regions of Thailand.

Production

Upstream activities. In terms of palm oil cultivators, approximately 0.24 million households across the country are involved in this sector, the majority (79%) of which are small holders. Larger estates typically invest in their own mills to extract crude palm oil.

Processing

Midstream activities. There are 149 mills in Thailand[15] of which 70% are in the southern provinces[16] with an estimated capacity to produce 2.8 million tons of crude palm oil per year. Larger mill operators are also investing in their own palm oil plantations and in developing new palm cultivars. The palm oil plant also produces a wide range of by-products that can generate additional income, such as kernel meal, which is used to manufacture animal feed, and palm shells and fiber which are used to produce biomass energy.

Downstream activities. There are 19 palm oil refineries in Thailand and the Office of Industrial Economics (OIE) estimates these refineries have an annual production capacity of 2.5 million tons. Large operators are often connected through investments in other parts of the palm oil supply chain such as crude palm oil mills and vegetable (edible) oils. Currently, the domestic palm oil refining capacity is insufficient to absorb the country's crude palm oil supply, and mills depend on several other industries to take up the balance. These industries include biodiesel, electricity and steam generation, biogas, and oil storage.

The palm oil supply chain of Thailand (Figure 1) starts from fresh palm oil that is obtained from fresh fruit bunch and loose fruit consisting of fresh palm oil, which undergo processing in palm oil mills for extraction. Around 38% of crude palm oil (CPO) will enter refinery plants to be extracted into refined palm oil (RPO), 94%; and palm fatty acid distill (PFAD), 33%. Of the final RPO demand, 9% is exported and 91% is for domestic consumption. Other refinery products include biodiesel, CPO for export, and CPO stock with the ratio of 31%, 11%, and 14%, respectively.

---

[15]   Krungsri Research 2020, Department of Industrial Works, and OIE.

[16]   Department of internal Trade, Ministry of Commerce. Map of Palm Oil Mill Operators. http://maps.dit.go.th/region/Report/rp_place_all.aspx?pid=31&poid=6&p=90.

Figure 1: Value Chain of Thailand Palm Oil Industry
(2018)

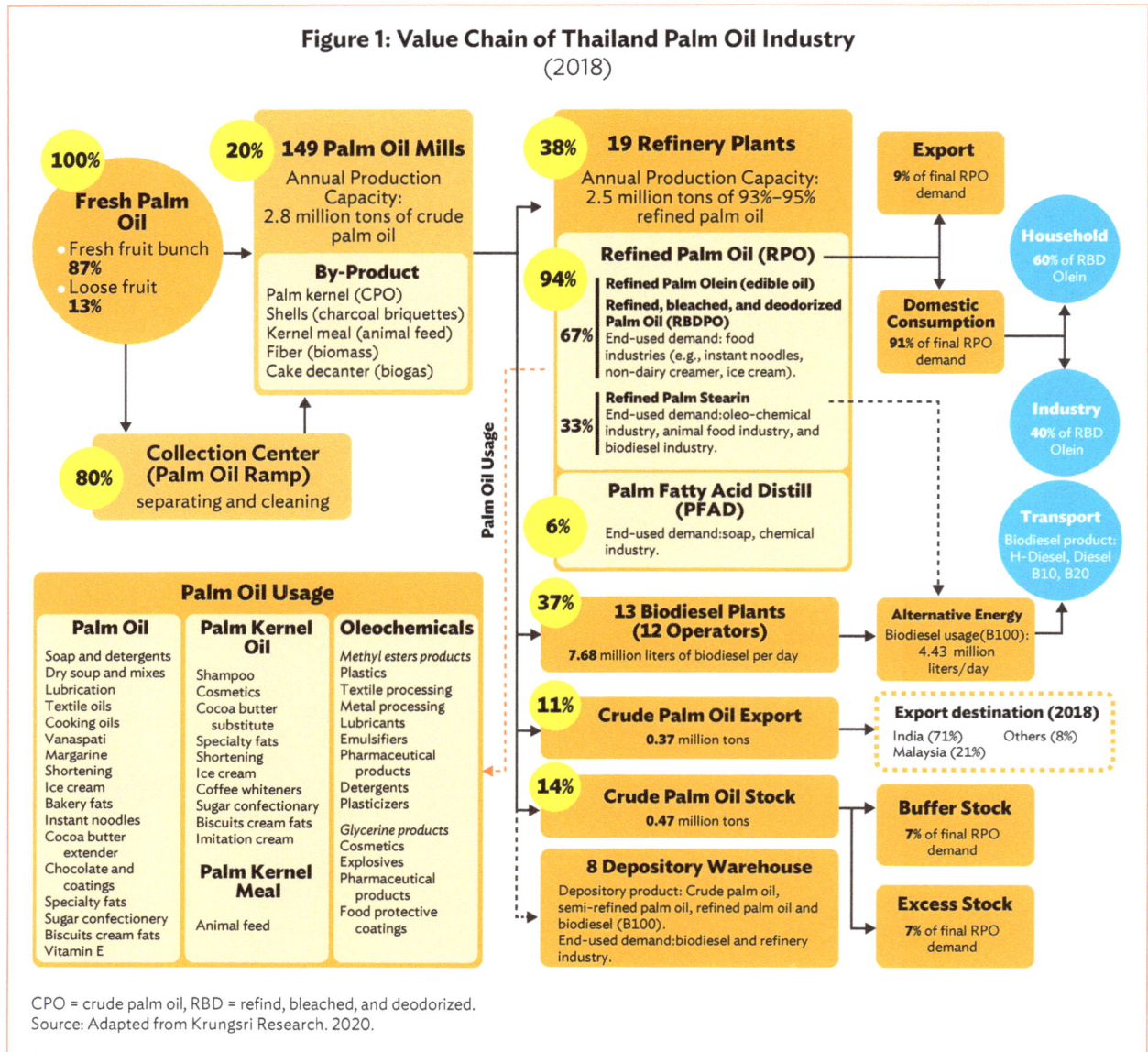

100%

Fresh Palm Oil
- Fresh fruit bunch **87%**
- Loose fruit **13%**

20%

149 Palm Oil Mills
Annual Production Capacity: 2.8 million tons of crude palm oil

By-Product
Palm kernel (CPO)
Shells (charcoal briquettes)
Kernel meal (animal feed)
Fiber (biomass)
Cake decanter (biogas)

80%

Collection Center (Palm Oil Ramp)
separating and cleaning

38%

19 Refinery Plants
Annual Production Capacity: 2.5 million tons of 93%–95% refined palm oil

Refined Palm Oil (RPO)

94%

Refined Palm Olein (edible oil)
Refined, bleached, and deodorized Palm Oil (RBDPO)
67% End-used demand: food industries (e.g., instant noodles, non-dairy creamer, ice cream).

Refined Palm Stearin
33% End-used demand: oleo-chemical industry, animal food industry, and biodiesel industry.

6%

Palm Fatty Acid Distill (PFAD)
End-used demand: soap, chemical industry.

Export
9% of final RPO demand

Domestic Consumption
91% of final RPO demand

Household
60% of RBD Olein

Industry
40% of RBD Olein

Transport
Biodiesel product: H-Diesel, Diesel B10, B20

Palm Oil Usage

37%

13 Biodiesel Plants (12 Operators)
7.68 million liters of biodiesel per day

Alternative Energy
Biodiesel usage(B100): 4.43 million liters/day

11%

Crude Palm Oil Export
0.37 million tons

Export destination (2018)
India (71%)   Others (8%)
Malaysia (21%)

14%

Crude Palm Oil Stock
0.47 million tons

8 Depository Warehouse
Depository product: Crude palm oil, semi-refined palm oil, refined palm oil and biodiesel (B100).
End-used demand: biodiesel and refinery industry.

Buffer Stock
7% of final RPO demand

Excess Stock
7% of final RPO demand

Palm Oil Usage

Palm Oil	Palm Kernel Oil	Oleochemicals
Soap and detergents	Shampoo	*Methyl esters products*
Dry soup and mixes	Cosmetics	Plastics
Lubrication	Cocoa butter substitute	Textile processing
Textile oils	Specialty fats	Metal processing
Cooking oils	Shortening	Lubricants
Vanaspati	Ice cream	Emulsifiers
Margarine	Coffee whiteners	Pharmaceutical products
Shortening	Sugar confectionary	Detergents
Ice cream	Biscuits cream fats	Plasticizers
Bakery fats	Imitation cream	
Instant noodles		*Glycerine products*
Cocoa butter extender	**Palm Kernel Meal**	Cosmetics
Chocolate and coatings		Explosives
Specialty fats	Animal feed	Pharmaceutical products
Sugar confectionery		Food protective coatings
Biscuits cream fats		
Vitamin E		

CPO = crude palm oil, RBD = refind, bleached, and deodorized.
Source: Adapted from Krungsri Research. 2020.

Distribution

The RPO distributed for domestic consumption goes to households (60%) and industrial users (40%). PFAD is used by the local chemical industry. The major export markets for CPO are India (71%) and Malaysia (21%). The destinations for the remaining 8% are Germany, the Lao PDR, and Singapore. Exports to India are transported through Laem Chabang Port and Singapore Port, while exports to Malaysia are transported by truck through Sadao BCP.

Palm Oil in Economic Corridor Provinces

Ninety percent of the total land area planted to palm oil in Thailand are in Southern Thailand. EC1 provinces account for 57% of plantation areas, followed by EC2 provinces with a share of 27%. Surat Thani accounts for almost half of the EC1 areas planted to palm oil. Palm oil mills are located mostly in Chumphon, Krabi, and Surat Thani, which are also the collection areas of fresh palm oil in the southern provinces. Fresh palm oil is transported to the mills and refineries in the central plains of Thailand. Seventy-five percent of CPO is used for the processing of downstream products such as edible oil, starch, and biodiesel (Table 42).

Table 42: Palm Oil Supply Chain in Economic Corridor Provinces in Thailand

Economic Corridor	Provinces	Palm Fruit Plantations			Processing	Distribution
		Area (hectares)	Production (Tons)	Share (%)	No. of Palm Oil Mills	
1	Songkhla	10,004	156,546	1.01	9	Refineries in Chumphon and BKK
	Surat Thani	188,713	3,640,097	23.43	34[a]	
	Nakhon Si Thammarat	84,809	1,553,088	10.00	9	
	Phatthalung	11,591	148,996	1.23	3	
	Chumphon	158,015	3,237,336	20.50	48[b]	
			Subtotal	56.71	100	Industrial estates and factories in BKK and vicinity
2	Krabi	173,790	3,383,122	21.78	42	
	Trang	30,718	556,291	3.58	7	
	Satun	17,322	276,557	1.78	7	
			Subtotal	27.14	56	
5	Ranong	19,048	366,956	2.36	3	Industrial estates and factories in Chonburi
	Phangnga	41,866	701,746	4.45	6	
	Phuket	325	4,593	0.03		
			Subtotal	6.84	10	
6	Pattani	2,923	45,772	0.29	1	
	Yala	1,168	10,574	0.12		11% (CPO) export to Germany, India, and Malaysia
	Narathiwat	8,570	108,426	0.70	1	
			Subtotal	1.11	2	
All ECs			Total	90.3	170	
All Southern			Total	90.03	170	
Others			Subtotal	9.97		
All Thailand			Total	100.00		

BKK = Bangkok, CPO = crude palm oil, EC = economic corridor.
[a] One refinery and one biodiesel.
[b] One refinery and one power plant.
Sources: Compiled by the author from: Office of Agricultural Economics, 2018. http://www.oae.go.th/assets/portals/1/fileups/prcaidata/files/oilpalm%2061.pdf; http://www.oae.go.th/assets/portals/1/files/ebook/2562/tradestat61.pdf; https://www.set.or.th/dat/news/201902/19015402.pdf.

Recommendations

The Government of Thailand has planned to develop Southern Thailand into a palm oil hub for trade and investment within the subregion. Most CPO exports from EC1 and EC2 provinces are transported by trucks to Laem Chabang deep seaport to be shipped via Singapore port to India, or other destination countries. There is a great potential to transport CPO from EC1 and EC2 through EC5 via Ranong deep seaport. If Ranong Port is utilized and developed to efficiently accommodate additional cargo volume, CPO from Ranong can be directly exported to India, Pakistan, and other destinations in South Asia. Transport costs and time will be significantly reduced, and product competitiveness will be improved.

Highways leading to gateway ports in EC5 must be upgraded to facilitate the transport of palm oil products across the corridor. More specifically, the following improvements should be undertaken:

(i)   Upgrade Highway No. 4 from Ranong (EC5) to Krabi (EC2) to four lanes;

(ii)   Upgrade Highway No. 4 to four lanes from Chumphon (EC1) to Ranong (EC5), connecting AH2 from central region via Highway No. 4 to Ranong Port;

(iii) Upgrade Ranong Port by investing in port equipment to facilitate goods handling and transport of CPO and other products from the economic corridors to India, Sri Lanka, or transshipment via India seaports to Africa, the Middle East, and Europe;

(iv)   Link Ranong Port with BIMSTEC subregion by implementing the memorandum of understanding between Ranong Port and Navayuga Container Terminal and Krishna Patnam Port, India.

Seventy-five percent of Thailand's palm oil industry consists of downstream activities. Thai investments in midstream and downstream industries in Sumatera will contribute to strengthening the palm oil industry value chain for Indonesia.

Rubber

Asian countries account for 90% of the world's production of natural rubber. Thailand is the world's major producer. In 2017, Thailand produced 4.42 million tons of natural rubber or 36% of global production, followed by Indonesia (26%), Viet Nam (8.6%), the PRC (8.0%), Malaysia (5.5%), and India (5.0%).

Natural Rubber Supply Chain in Thailand

Production

Thailand ranks second in the world in terms of land area planted to rubber, following Indonesia's lead. In 2017, the total rubber plantation areas in Thailand were 3.60 million hectares. Sixty percent of rubber plantation areas are situated in the south, followed by the northeast with 23%; the central plains with 11% and the north with 6%.

Thailand is the world's number one producer and exporter of natural rubber. In 2017, Thailand produced 4.42 million tons of natural rubber, 83% of which was exported, with the remaining 17% going to domestic consumption. In terms of intermediate processed rubber, Thailand produces most of technically specified rubber, followed by concentrated latex, mixture, ribbed smoked sheet (RSS), and other types of rubber such as compound rubber.

Processing

Upstream activities. The upstream industry involves rubber farmers and rubber tappers. Some farmers have started to participate in rubber processing to add value to the primary production. Most of Thailand's primary production is used as inputs into the domestic intermediate industry and the rest for export. The primary product is tapped rubber, 100% of which are processed into three products:

(i)   Latex (59%). Farmers tend to sell latex more for convenience and for hedging against the risk of price fluctuation.

(ii)   Raw rubber sheet (8%). The rubber sheet produced by farmers are not smoked or processed by any other means.

(iii)   Cup lump or rubber crumb (33%). The tapped rubber is latex that, when mixed with chemicals, will become coagulated rubber. The production of cup lump by farmers has increased in many areas especially in Surat Thani, Pattani, Yala, and Narathiwat. Cup lump is an alternative for farmers in the south as it is easily produced, economical, consumes less time, and not labor-intensive. Quality cup lump is in the form of a cup, clean, beautiful color, without contaminants or foul order, with the weight of approximately 80 grams–500 grams.

Intermediate activities. The intermediate industry involves processors of natural rubber. The rubber from plantations are processed into semi-finished products such as RSS, technically specified rubber (TSR), or standard Thai rubber (STR), concentrated latex, compound rubber, and skim rubber with necessary qualifications for domestic and international downstream producers. Upstream products used as raw material for rubber product industries include concentrated latex, RSS, and TSR, among others. The products are divided into four types: TSR (41%), raw rubber sheet (38%), concentrated latex (20%), and crape rubber (1%).

Downstream activities. The downstream industry involves processing intermediate products into final products for consumers (Figure 2). The final products include pillows, latex mattresses, rubber gloves, condoms, rubber roads, auto tires, motorcycle tires, aircraft tires, rubber bands, conveyor belts, athletic shoes, waterproof strips, and others. In some cases, synthetic rubber, which is developed from the petrochemical sector, is an alternative to natural rubber or mixed with natural rubber to enhance qualities depending on the function or use. Figure 3 shows Thailand's rubber products supply chain. Figure 4 shows the distribution of rubber products to various export markets.

Figure 2: Thailand's Rubber Supply Chain

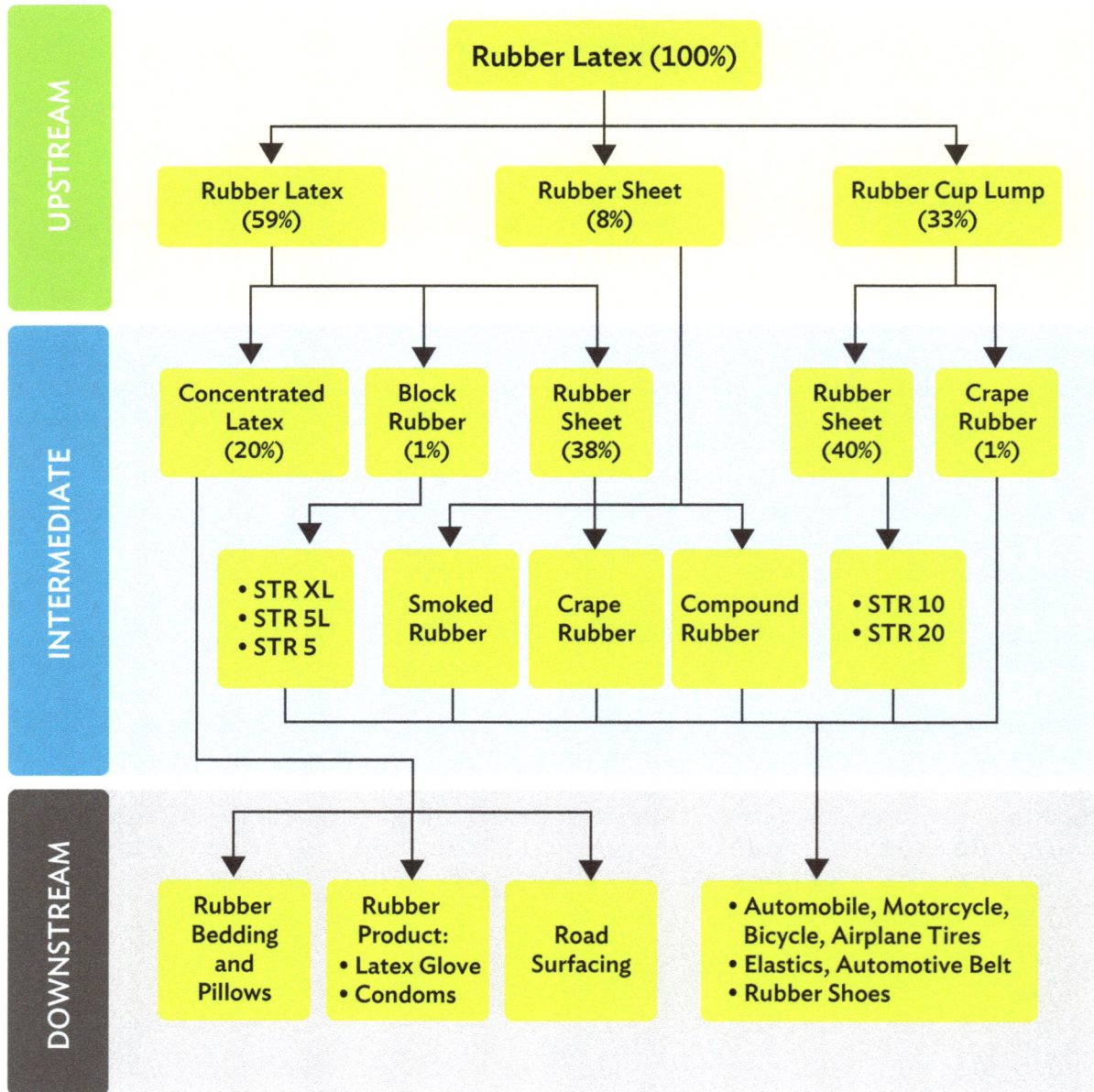

STR = standard Thai rubber.
Sources: Bank of Thailand, Customs, 2016.

Figure 3: Thailand's Rubber Products Supply Chain

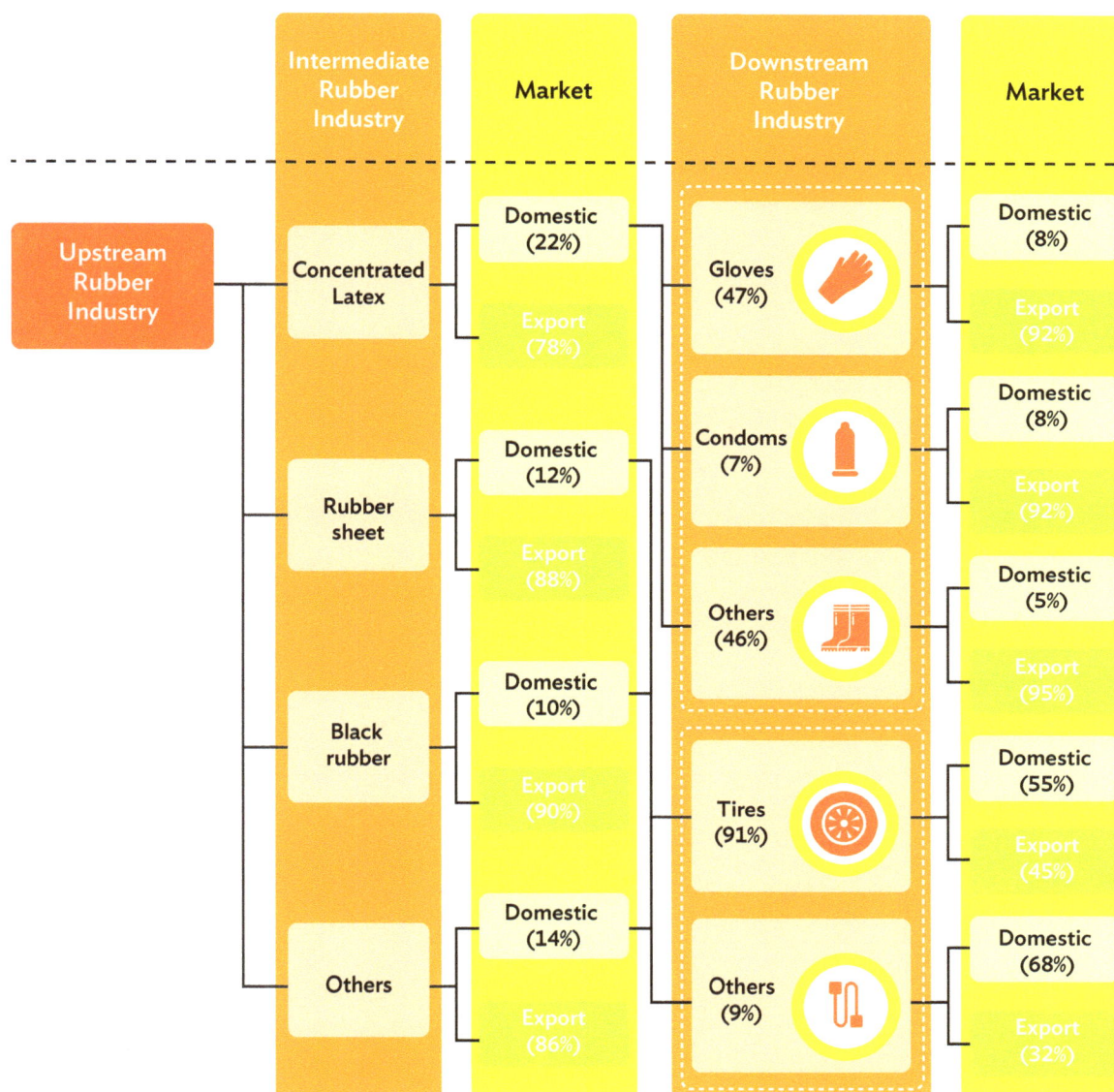

Source: Office of Industrial Economics. Adapted from Krungsri Research.

Rubber latex. Rubber latex is exported to the PRC (56%), Malaysia (14%), European Union (7%), Japan (5%), the United States (5%), and the Republic of Korea (3%) (Figure 5). Exports of rubber latex contribute approximately 78% of Thailand's exports of rubber products, which are divided into two groups: (i) semi-finished rubber products or primary processed rubber products, which are outputs from the processing of tapped latex in various forms to be used as raw materials in the rubber product industry; and (ii) rubber finished products which include auto tires, rubber gloves, condoms, conveyor belts, rubber pipes, etc.

Figure 4: Thailand's Rubber Latex Supply Chain and Distribution

Rubber Latex (100%)

Stock (9.2%)

Export (78.8%)

Domestic Consumption (12.0%)

People's Republic of China (56%)

Malaysia (14%)

European Union (7%)

Japan (5%)

United States (5%)

Republic of Korea (3%)

Compound Rubber (4.7%)

Block Rubber (39.4%)

Smoked Rubber (12.9%)

Concentrated Latex (25.7%)

Mixture (16.0%)

People's Republic of China (75%)

People's Republic of China (100%)

People's Republic of China (62%)

European Union (10%)

Republic of Korea (6%)

United States (5%)

Malaysia (49%)

People's Republic of China (33%)

European Union (3%)

Republic of Korea (3%)

People's Republic of China (26%)

Japan (21%)

European Union (14%)

United States (14%)

Sources: Bank of Thailand, Customs, and Ministry of Agriculture 2016.

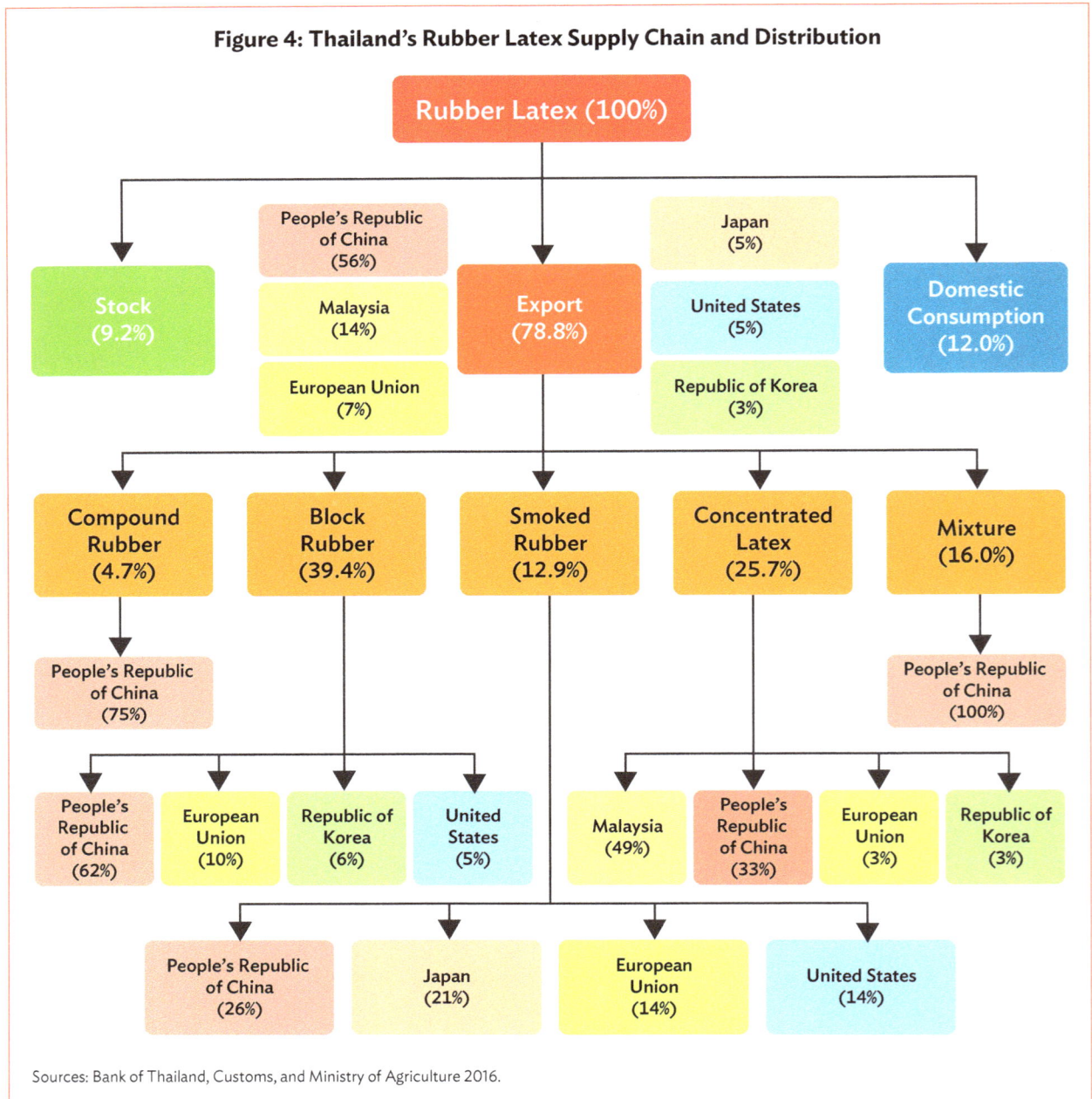

The distribution of rubber and rubber products use both maritime and land transport.

Around one-third (34%) of rubber exports go through Laem Chabang Port. Rubber products from factories are transported by land to the coastal port of Surat Thani to Laem Chabang Port for shipment to export destinations. Kantang Port (3%) and Songkhla Port (3%) are used to transport TSR, RSS, concentrated latex, compound rubber, and mixture to Penang Port and Singapore Port from which these products are exported to other destinations. Phuket Port (1%) is also used.

As regards land-based distribution, about (33%) of products from factories are transported through Padang Besar BCP to Penang Port to Singapore Port for exports to destination countries. Fourteen percent are transported through Sadao BCP for exports to Malaysia. Chiang Khong or Chiang Saen BCP (1%) are used to transport rubber products to Sieng Kong Pier (Lao PDR), and Sop Loei Pier (Myanmar) for exports to the PRC.

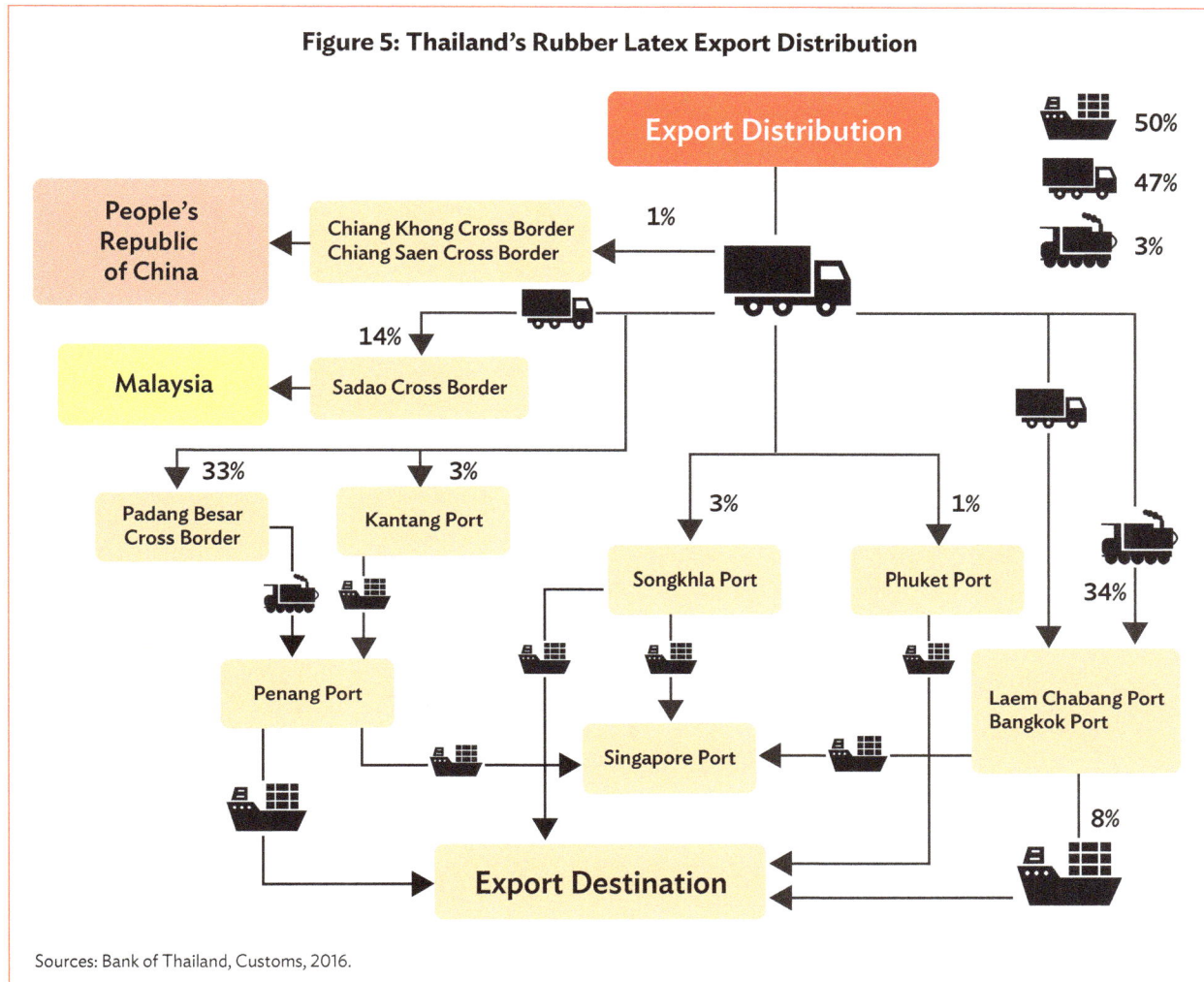

Figure 5: Thailand's Rubber Latex Export Distribution

Sources: Bank of Thailand, Customs, 2016.

Rubber in Economic Corridor Provinces

Rubber is an economic crop that is crucial to the economy of Southern Thailand. It generates revenue for the country and increases farmers' income. The south is situated in a tropical zone, which is suitable for rubber cultivation than other regions and accounts for 60% of the total rubber plantation areas in the country. The rubber plantation areas of provinces that are part of the IMT-GT economic corridors constitute 53.7% of the rubber plantation areas nationwide. EC1 provinces contribute 30%; EC2, 10.7%; EC5, 1.6%; and EC6, 11.2%. The development of rubber supply chain will be particularly important for EC1 and EC6 that collect, process, and distribute rubber products for domestic consumption and export (Table 43).

Table 43: Rubber Supply Chain in Economic Corridor Provinces in Thailand

Economic Corridor	Provinces	Rubber Plantations			Processing	Distribution
		Area (hectares)	Production (tons)	Share (%)		
1	Songkhla	316,599	410,402	8.47	1. Natural rubber • concentrate latex • ribbed smoked sheet • air-dried sheets • block rubber • crepes rubber • skim rubber 2. Synthetic rubber 3. Rubber gloves 4. Condom 5. Latex pillow 6. Rubber shoes 7. Prayer mat 8. Rubber flooring 9. Balloon	**EC1:** Borders • Sadao BC • Padang Besar BC • Ban Prakop BC Ports • Penang Port • Port Klang • Songkhla Port • Coastal pier, Surat Thani go to Laem Chabang Port
	Surat Thani	407,113	547,211	11.29		
	Nakhon Si Thammarat	240,052	389,280	8.03		
	Chumphon	83,895	123,081	2.32		
			Subtotal	**30.11**		
2	Krabi	89,445	131,669	2.47	1. Natural rubber • concentrate latex • ribbed smoked sheet • air-dried sheets • block rubber • crepes rubber • skim rubber 2. Pillow for health 3. Bull pillow, air-dried sheets pillow 4. Latex mattress 5. Sandals / Boots 6. Other products • Carambola helps washing clothes wonders • Rubber outsole • Flooring rubber • Rubber squeeze ball for exercise • Frog fins from rubber • Gloves • Carrying bag	**EC2:** Ports • Penang Port • Port Klang • Laem Chabang Port **EC5:** Ports • Phuket Port • Laem Chabang Port **EC6:** Borders • Su-ngai Kolok BC • Tak Bai BC • Buketa BC • Betong BC 1. Natural rubber • concentrate latex • ribbed smoked sheet • air-dried sheets • block rubber • crepes rubber • skim rubber 2. Synthetic rubber 3. Rubber gloves
	Trang	233,154	328,897	6.44		
	Satun	67,449	89,933	1.86		
			Subtotal	**10.77**		
5	Ranong	49,856	65,982	1.36	1. Natural rubber • concentrate latex • ribbed smoked sheet • air-dried sheets • block rubber • crepes rubber • skim rubber	
	Phuket	10,738	12,726	0.26		
			Subtotal	**1.62**		

continued on next page

Table 43 (continued)

Economic Corridor	Provinces	Rubber Plantations			Processing	Distribution
		Area (hectares)	Production (tons)	Share (%)		
6	Pattani	59,192	84,238	1.74	1. Natural rubber	**Export to 78.8%**
	Yala	199,718	261,043	5.39	• concentrate latex	• PRC
					• ribbed smoked sheet	• Malaysia
					• air-dried sheets	• EU
					• block rubber	• Japan
					• crepes rubber	• US
					• skim rubber	
					2. Latex pillow	
	Narathiwat	161,141	197,937	4.09	3. Rubber shoes	
					4. Heel rubber	
					5. Rubber sponge	
					6. Rubber products	
					• Rubber band	
					3. Finished rubber (rubber mixed with chemicals)	
			Subtotal	**11.22**	4. Power wash ball	
All Economic Corridors			**Total**	**53.72**		
Others	Phatthalung	142,291	210,694	3.93		
	Phangnga	99,624	146,367	2.75		
			Subtotal	**6.68**		
Southern			**Total**	**60.40**		
Other			**Total**	**39.60**		
Thailand			**Total**	**100.00**		

BC = border crossing, EC = economic corridor, EU = European Union, PRC = People's Republic of China, US = United States.
Sources: Compiled by the author from: Office of Agricultural Economics, 2018. http://www.oae.go.th/assets/portals/1/files/ebook/2562/tradestat61.pdf (accessed 30 September 2020); http://www.oae.go.th/assets/portals/1/fileups/prcaidata/files/oilpalm%2061.pdf (accessed 30 September 2020); https://www.set.or.th/dat/news/201902/19015402.pdf (accessed 30 September 2020).

Thailand promotes foreign direct investment in the rubber industry by providing incentives according to the criteria of the Board of Investment of Thailand and the Rubber City project that has been established in Songkhla under the IMT-GT with priority to developing rubber innovation and an integrated rubber industry. The government is actively searching for partnerships in the international rubber market to turn Thailand into an original equipment manufacturer (OEM).[17] Thailand's comparative advantage in rubber production gives it the potential to become an OEM center where rubber entrepreneurs can cater to demands of importers worldwide, which could ultimately impact on the stability of domestic rubber prices.

---

[17] An OEM is a fully integrated firm that designs, manufactures, and sells its brands under registered trademarks.

Findings and Recommendations

The Government of Thailand should continue to develop the southern region to become a rubber industry hub by promoting the IMT-GT Rubber City in Songkhla where investments have been accorded privileges especially those that are geared toward downstream products.

Indonesia, Malaysia, and Thailand can upgrade and integrate the value chain of rubber by focusing on research and development, and sharing innovations across upstream, intermediate, and downstream industries. The objective is long-term value creation and employment generation, benefiting the development of IMT-GT economic corridors.

The reconfigured EC1, EC5, and the new EC6 will cover a wider area of rubber supply chain activities in IMT-GT. The new EC6 will support cross-border supply chains along the border in the eastern region of Thailand and Malaysia where rubber production and rubber products manufacturing are mostly concentrated. Moreover, the new EC6 will connect multimodal logistics systems (road, rail, and waterway) that will promote greater industrial efficiency and viability that can lead to job creation and income generation for the local community.

EC1 currently serves as a strategic gateway for transporting rubber and the proposed EC6 has a great potential to become a major gateway as well. A number of physical connectivity projects (PCPs) has been prioritized by IMT-GT to promote multimodal connectivity in these two corridors covering roads, rails, seaports, airports, CIQ facilities, SEZs, ICDs and relevant logistics facilities.

Halal Food

Thailand is ranked as the world's seventh and Asia's first as producer and exporter of agricultural products and food.[18] Thailand's policy environment as well as natural endowments are key factors that enable the country to exploit its full potential as a major producer and exporter of agricultural products and food such as fishery (shrimps and fish), chicken, rice, and canned pineapples. Thailand is the world's number one exporter of shrimps and the world's number three exporter of fish and seafood, following the PRC and Norway.

The export of Thailand's halal food is still small—less than 1% compared to the total value of Thailand's food exports. Thailand's comparative advantage in agriculture and food production and the high demand for halal food in the global market offer a tremendous opportunity for Thailand to develop its halal food industry. The key challenge is to develop and diversify production in line with the needs of the market to expand exports and ultimately realize the country's vision to be the "Kitchen of the World."

In 2017, there were 4,683 halal-certified companies by the Central Islamic Council of Thailand compared to 2,188 companies in 1999—an increase of 114%. Around 99% of the halal-certified companies were involved in food production. These include food producers, 72%; restaurants, 13%; slaughterhouses, 3%; food importers, 2%; and the remaining 10% are producers or importers consumer products such as cosmetics, toothpaste, medicine, or herbs, etc.

---

[18]   Other major producers and exporters are Australia, Brazil, Canada, European Union, the PRC, and United States. Thai Halal Standard: Promote Halal export opportunity to Halal market, 2008. https://positioningmag.com/39961.

Thailand's Halal Supply Chain

Production

The preparation, production, packaging, storage, distribution, maintenance of food safety, marks, and labels that comply with standards create confidence among consumers about the quality of halal food. Because standards of halal food vary worldwide, it is important that halal standards are traceable. For instance, raw materials in raising livestock must comply with the required standards that are traceable and based on Good Agricultural Practice for Farm Animals. A significant portion of the population in EC1 and EC2 (Songkhla, Satun, Pattani, Narathiwat, and Yala) are converts of Islam and strict Islamic practices are different from other areas in the country. It is therefore important to build trust and confidence of consumers in these areas. Animal farm operators who are not converts of Islam should take Islamic practices into account by adhering to the standards required for the certification process to foster confidence in their products.[19] It is important to comply with the strict standards of halal food production process from upstream to downstream activities with attention to detail and prudence in each process to ensure safety of the consumers and the products (Figure 6).

Figure 6: Thailand's Halal Supply Chain

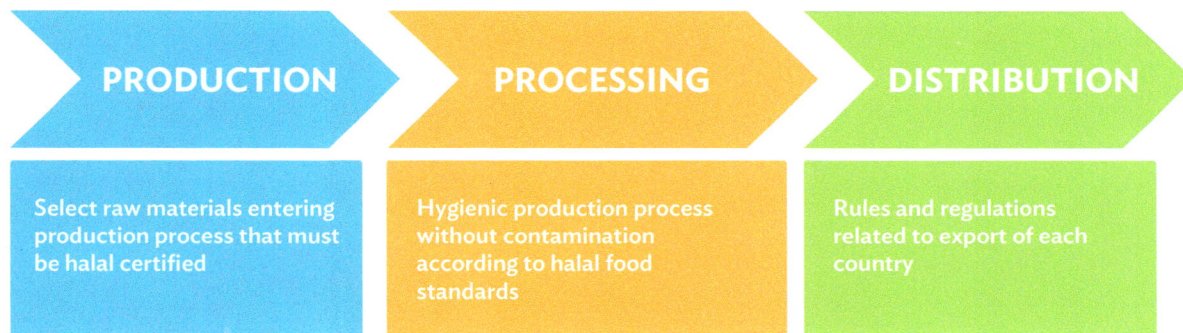

PRODUCTION	PROCESSING	DISTRIBUTION
Select raw materials entering production process that must be halal certified	Hygienic production process without contamination according to halal food standards	Rules and regulations related to export of each country

Source: Compiled by the author.

Processing

The production process starts by buying raw materials from suppliers who present the goods and documents accompanying the standards of safety of consumption and documents certifying the raw materials with the halal. The documents can be used to request for approval of the halal marks, which are the company's products if the raw materials in the production have the documents certifying the halal marks in every raw material during storage and transport, which must be separated from the other prohibited food and must not be contaminated with non-halal composition.

---

[19] C. Wattanachan. 2012. *Halal Production and Processing Process.* https://ag2.kku.ac.th/kaj/PDF.cfm?filename=204.pdf&id=687&keeptrack=6.

Distribution

In the past, the export of Thailand's halal food was approximately $5.8 billion in 2017 (or up 12.5% year-on-year).[20] The major export markets included ASEAN countries especially Indonesia and Malaysia, and the Middle East. The ASEAN countries where there are many Muslims are Brunei Darussalam, Indonesia, Malaysia, and Singapore. Indonesia is a growing market of halal food. It is a country with the highest Muslim population in the world. The Muslim population in Indonesia is approximately 200 million or over 84% of Indonesia's total population of approximately 237 million. The demand to consume halal-certified products is on the rise, especially because of the 115 million middle class Indonesians or 45% of Indonesia's total population with the purchasing power. Indonesia does not produce sufficient food for domestic demand so it must import meat, livestock, and milk. In 2006, the import of halal goods of Indonesia was valued at approximately $6.2 billion. It is expected that the Thailand's export of halal food to Indonesia will experience high growth and Thai exporters of halal food will benefit from tax incentives under the ASEAN Free Trade Area (Figure 7).

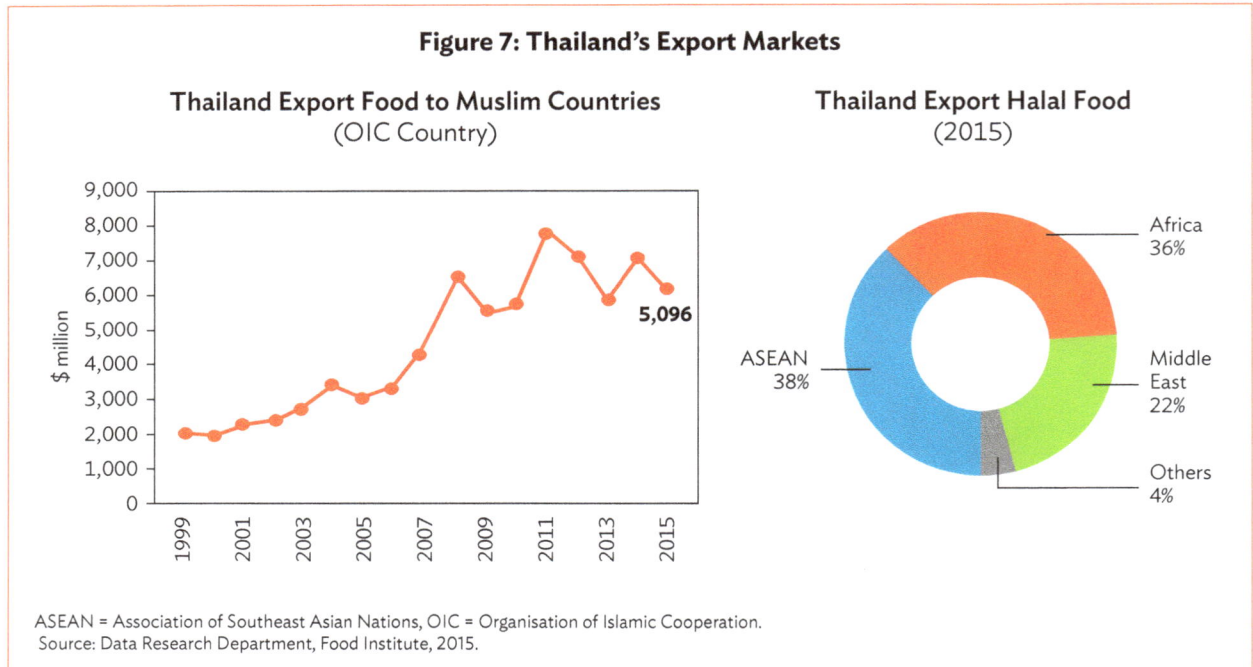

Figure 7: Thailand's Export Markets

ASEAN = Association of Southeast Asian Nations, OIC = Organisation of Islamic Cooperation.
Source: Data Research Department, Food Institute, 2015.

The main export products remain natural halal food such as rice, sugar, tapioca flour, processed seafood, canned fruits and vegetables, and fresh and processed chicken. The latest information of the global halal food market reveals that Thailand is ranked 10th in the world as exporter of halal food to Muslim countries with the export value of approximately $6 billion or 3.7% of the total trade value of food in Muslim countries and with growth of 8% for the past 5 years. The leading exporters of halal food to Muslim markets include India with a global share of 9.4%, followed by Brazil (8.3%), the United States (6.7%), the Russian Federation (5.5%), and the PRC (4.8%), all of which are non-Muslim countries.

---

[20]   Kasikorn Thai Research Center. 2018. SME Analysis. *Thai SME for Halal Market.* https://www.kasikornbank.com/th/business/sme/KSMEKnowledge/article/KSMEAnalysis/Documents/Thai-SME-Opportunity_Halal-Market.pdf.

Halal in Economic Corridor Provinces

Halal food is promoted in the south border provinces of Pattani, Yala, Narathiwat, Satun, and Songkhla situated in EC1, EC2, and EC6 with a combined population of approximately 3.6 million, which 62% are Muslims. Provinces with the highest Muslim populations are Narathiwat (86%), Pattani (81%), Yala (77%), Satun (74%), and Songkhla (33%).[21] The government's policy is to develop these provinces as the center of production and exportation of halal food in Thailand. The government is in the process of establishing the Halal Food Industrial Estate in Pattani. Many provinces in the south produce abundant raw materials for halal food production such as marine animals and seafood and livestock such as goat, sheep, cow, and buffalo.

There are 370 establishments and 813 products that have registered for the certification of halal standards.[22] The establishments are of two types, private halal food business establishments (or SMEs), and halal food community enterprises (housewife groups) (Table 44).

Table 44: Number of Business Establishments of Halal Food in the Southern Border Provinces

Province	Community Enterprises	SMEs	Total
Pattani	26	66	92
Yala	107	48	155
Narathiwat	6	16	22
Songkhla	29	23	52
Satun	20	29	49
Total	**118**	**182**	**370**

SMEs = small and medium-sized enterprises.
Source: Islamic Council of Pattani, Yala, and Narathiwat, 2013. Songkhla and Satun data compiled by the author.

The status of investment in halal food business in the south border provinces reveals that in Pattani, there are six large factories in seafood processing and one large factory in Narathiwat. In Yala, there is no large factory, only SMEs. Yala has the highest share of community enterprises, followed by Pattani and Narathiwat (Table 45). The major factor for investment in halal food business is resources. Pattani is the center of seafood trade, so the main investment is in seafood processing. Yala is mainly engaged in agriculture, so the main investment is in agricultural processing. Narathiwat is the province bordering Malaysia with the highest number of BCPs so the main investment is in halal food business for export.

Table 45: Number of Halal Food Products in the Southern Border Provinces

Province	Community Enterprises	SMEs	Total
Pattani	53	153	206
Yala	303	86	389
Narathiwat	8	22	30
Songkhla	43	72	115
Satun	52	21	73
Total	**459**	**354**	**813**

SMEs = small and medium-sized enterprises.
Source: Islamic Council of Pattani, Yala and Narathiwat. 2013.

---

21   The Halal Science Center, Chulalongkorn University. 2019. https://bit.ly/HalalKitchensInSouthernBorderProvinces.

22   I. Darakai, A. Yusoh, K. Botlum, and Y. Dorlee. 2013. *The Halal Food Business Investment in Southern Border Province of Thailand A Case Study: Pattani, Yala, and Narathiwat Provinces.* Phatthalung: Thaksin University.

As Thailand is not a Muslim country, the reliability of Thailand's halal food certification standards from the perspective of Muslim consumers differs from how they perceive the standards of Muslim halal food exporters from Malaysia and Indonesia. As a result, Malaysia's halal food certification labels receive more confidence and recognition than Thailand's halal product certification labels.

The strict inspection and certification of quality halal food in terms of standards of halal food production, standards of inspection of halal certification by assessors, and standards of halal-certified bodies are important measures that the Central Islamic Committee of Thailand must use to set up common standards for halal certification or accreditation in the country and pursue international standard. Certification is a major factor that supports Thailand's halal food exports in meeting international halal food quality standards in the world market.

Malaysia has its advantage in export of halal food, as it is a Muslim country.[23] Subsequently, Malaysia's halal food certification marks are recognized worldwide. Malaysia formulates the policy to promote the production of halal food for export and plans to set up the Halal Food Industrial Estate in the north of the country near the Thai border with Songkhla. At the same time, Thailand is setting up the Halal Food Industrial Estate in Pattani. Malaysia's halal food products are world-renowned. Thailand is also advantageous in terms of modern and advanced food production. Moreover, Thailand is a net exporter of food with domestic raw material sources while Malaysia is a net importer of food. Malaysia's import value of food is over $3.2 billion a year. Malaysia's net imported goods include meat and goat. In addition, Indonesia, Malaysia, and Thailand cooperate under the IMT-GT with the cooperative policy to develop halal food standards for the recognition of halal food products in the world market. Malaysia and Indonesia are Muslim countries and should cooperate and promote the export of Thailand as IMT-GT halal food products for wider recognition in the global market.

Findings and Recommendations

Thailand has a great opportunity to become a supplier and producer of halal products. With the new EC6, it will be possible to have a more integrated halal food cross-border value chain between Thailand and Malaysia. To support further integration of the value chain in Malaysia and Thailand, the following spatial connectivity improvements would be needed:

(i)   Construction of the bridge over Kolok River at Tak Bai–Pengkalan Kubur connecting Tak Bai and cities in Kelantan State. The bridge will facilitate the movement of Malaysian visitors to Pattani Narathiwat and Songkhla to purchase halal food, and will establish an alternative export channel to Indonesia and Malaysia.

(ii)   Establishment of the Narathiwat SEZ to promote and attract investments in processed halal food industries and create a better link between raw materials supply and processing facilities.

(iii)   Provision of support to the Southern Border Provinces Administrative Center (SBPAC) development of halal logistics system in the southern border provinces to prepare for the economic expansion in the Deep South.

At the subregional level, Indonesia, Malaysia, and Thailand are collaborating to harmonize halal standards to come up with a unified IMT-GT halal brand globally. This is one of the cooperation objectives in the IMT-GT Implementation Blueprint 2017–2021, which is under the purview of the IMT-GT working group on halal products and services.

---

[23]   SME Knowledge Center. 2018. https://www.sme.go.th/upload/mod_download/download-20181005063632.pdf.

ADDRESSING GAPS IN INSTITUTIONAL MECHANISMS FOR ECONOMIC CORRIDOR DEVELOPMENT

Thailand's Institutional Coordinating Mechanisms

The implementation of the IMT-GT road map requires close cooperation and coordination between relevant agencies, both the public and the private sectors. The private sector is envisaged to drive the economy of the subregion with the public sector providing the appropriate policy environment as well as the basic infrastructure to support the private sector operations. The roles of the public and the private sectors are complementary. National coordinating mechanisms thus play a crucial role in implementing the IMT-GT blueprints among various stakeholders at all levels to achieve desired goals.[24]

National Coordination Mechanisms

In Thailand, all projects concerning the development along IMT-GT economic corridors are perceived as vital to overall development of IMT-GT. Decisions on these projects are made at the highest level involving the prime minister and the Cabinet (Figure 8).

The secretary-general of the Office of the National Economic and Social Development Council (NESDC) is the senior official-in-charge IMT-GT cooperation, reporting to the deputy prime minister (DPM) in charge of economic affairs. The DPM authorizes the matters to be presented to the secretary-general of the Cabinet. The secretariat of the Cabinet circulates the matters to all agencies concerned for their views and comments that will guide the Cabinet in making the final decisions.

NESDC consults closely with the IMT-GT minister before the annual ministerial meeting. For matters needing Cabinet resolution, NESDC will propose directly to the DPM. The minister of transport who is the IMT-GT minister submits their opinion to the secretariat of the Cabinet, together with all other relevant ministries.

The present IMT-GT minister is the minister of finance, who is responsible for all PCPs in IMT-GT. The IMT-GT budget utilized for PCPs has the biggest stake for IMT-GT compared with other areas of cooperation. During each annual ministerial meeting, the minister of finance may authorize the deputy minister to be the alternate IMT-GT minister.

Senior Level

The IMT-GT minister is selected by the Cabinet. When starting the project, the minister of transport is the IMT-GT minister, which is then changed to the minister of finance.

The secretary-general (DSG) makes decisions on their behalf or can be the head of delegation during Senior Officials Meetings (SOMs), as the alternate senior official. The DSG may also authorize the senior advisor to act on their behalf.

The DSG conducts internal preparatory meetings for Thailand's positions on matters to be discussed at the IMT-GT meeting. The national secretariat prepares the groundwork for this meeting, including the drafting of relevant strategies based on Thailand's National Economic and Social Development Plan, 20-Year National Strategy, and other Cabinet resolutions and policies relevant to IMT-GT. Strategies, decisions, and work plans

---

24   Chiraphat Chotipimai, NESDC, July 2020.

of working groups, the Chief Ministers and Governors Forum (CMGF) Secretariat for Thailand, the Joint Business Council (JBC), and the Centre For IMT-GT Subregional Cooperation are also considered by the national secretariat in preparing the documents for the internal preparatory meetings.

Figure 8: Thailand's Institutional Coordinating Mechanisms Structure

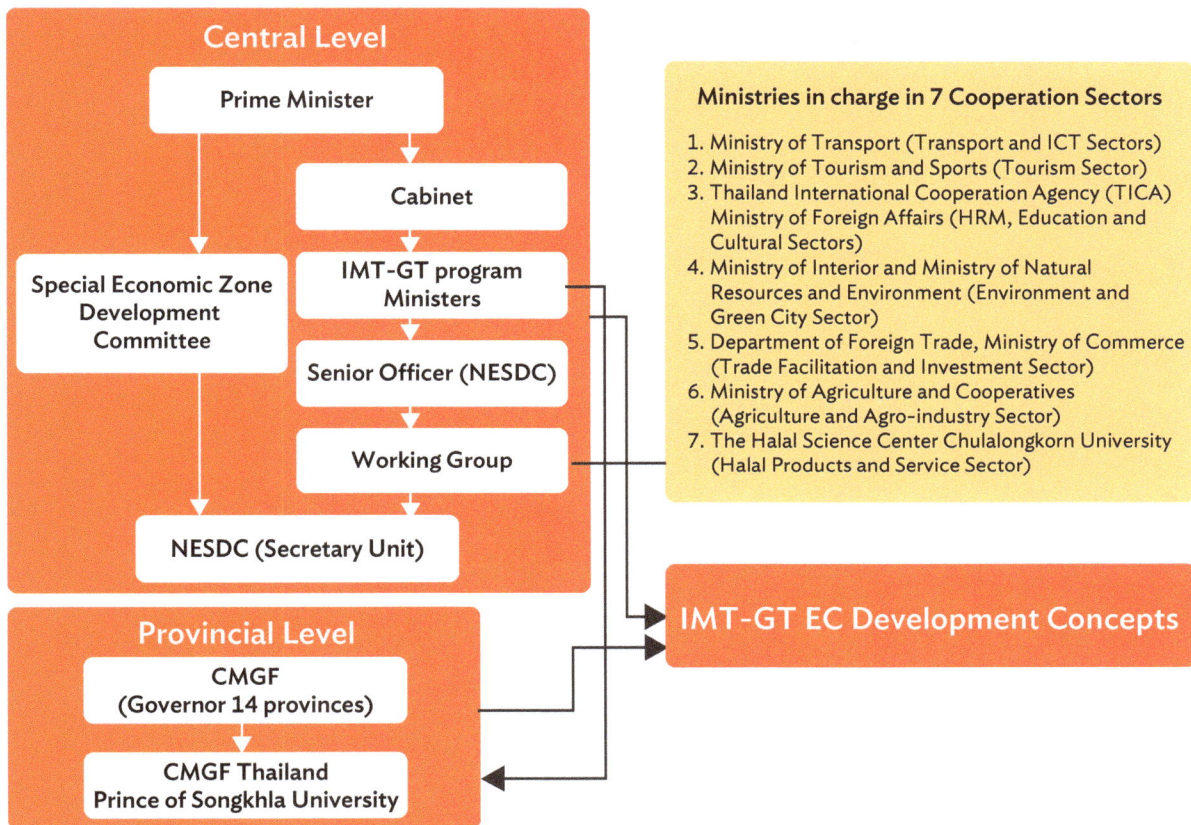

Central Level

Prime Minister

Cabinet

Special Economic Zone Development Committee

IMT-GT program Ministers

Senior Officer (NESDC)

Working Group

NESDC (Secretary Unit)

Provincial Level

CMGF (Governor 14 provinces)

CMGF Thailand Prince of Songkhla University

Ministries in charge in 7 Cooperation Sectors

1. Ministry of Transport (Transport and ICT Sectors)
2. Ministry of Tourism and Sports (Tourism Sector)
3. Thailand International Cooperation Agency (TICA) Ministry of Foreign Affairs (HRM, Education and Cultural Sectors)
4. Ministry of Interior and Ministry of Natural Resources and Environment (Environment and Green City Sector)
5. Department of Foreign Trade, Ministry of Commerce (Trade Facilitation and Investment Sector)
6. Ministry of Agriculture and Cooperatives (Agriculture and Agro-industry Sector)
7. The Halal Science Center Chulalongkorn University (Halal Products and Service Sector)

IMT-GT EC Development Concepts

CMGF = Chief Ministers and Governors Forum, EC = economic corridor, HRM = human resource management, ICT = information and communication technology, IMT-GT = Indonesia–Malaysia–Thailand Growth Triangle, NESDC = National Economic and Social Development Council.
Source: National Economic and Social Development Council, 2020.

The lead roles performed at different levels are as follows:

(i)   Ministerial meetings: The Cabinet will assign the relevant minister to be the IMT-GT minister.

(ii)   SOM: NESDC secretary-general will be assigned or will assign the DSG or senior advisor as alternate to attend the meeting.

(iii)   National Secretariat: The director of International Strategy and Coordination Division or the head of IMT-GT Unit under the division will be assigned as alternate to attend the meeting.

The official mandate of these officials will be covered by a special letter or administrative letter of appointment in their designated position. At ministerial meetings, the NESDC will have to get the relevant Cabinet resolution for each IMT-GT minister. At the senior officials' level, the appointment will depend on the authority of DSG in charge of the International Strategy and Coordination Office. At the national secretariat level, the appointment will depend on the person-in-charge of the IMT-GT Unit.

The designated focal persons to handle the IMT-GT and other programs as follows:

(i)   Ministerial meetings: IMT-GT and GMS;

(ii)   Senior Officials: IMT-GT, the Thailand–Malaysia Committee on Joint Development Strategy for Border Areas (JDS), Greater Mekong Subregion (GMS), Asia-Pacific Economic Cooperation (APEC), and Organisation for Economic Co-operation and Development (OECD), ASEAN; and

(iii)   National Secretariat: IMT-GT, JDS and other bilateral cooperation.

Three dedicated staff assist the national secretariat and senior officials for IMT-GT, JDS, and ASEAN.

Coordination with Line Ministries

NESDC as central focal agency coordinates with the line ministries. This mandate is contained in a Cabinet resolution tasking NESDC to monitor the progress and coordinate relevant strategies for IMT-GT. The line ministries assign focal points for IMT-GT.

Preparatory interagency meetings before all ministerial meetings and SOM are arranged by NESDC. Working group leaders also arrange for preparatory meetings. The CMGF and JBC are also involved. The CMGF arranges for an annual seminar for the staff of 14 provinces to prepare project proposals to be presented to the annual CMGF.

The flow of information between the central agency and the line ministries is through NESDC as national coordinator. The lead agencies of the working groups will also coordinate with relevant agencies and sometimes arrange relevant meetings in the working groups to follow up after all IMT-GT agencies have discussed with NESDC.

The line ministries also coordinate with their counterparts at the provinces and states in every working group, especially ministries that have their provincial units in the 14 southern provinces. This coordination is conducted by consultation with NESDC before every meeting of the working group, the CMGF, and JBC. Information flow is always two-way.

One improvement that can be made in the coordination mechanism between the central agencies and line and sectoral ministries is the establishment of project implementation teams composed of agencies involved in implementing a project. Although this mechanism has been agreed upon by the IMT-GT, the project implementation teams have not been set in place.

Coordination with the Provincial Government

The coordination mechanism for IMT-GT activities at the provincial level is led by CMGF (Thailand) utilizing staff from the Prince of Songkhla University funded by Ministry of Interior. The line of communication between provinces and the central government is from NESDC to Ministry of Interior to CMGF Secretariat (Thailand) and all 14 provinces.

The NESDC, by virtue of its mandate, informs the provinces of decisions by the IMT-GT ministers, senior officials, the CMGF, working groups, and the special planning meeting pertaining to the economic corridors.

Local governments and the SBPAC are involved in the planning and implementation of corridor projects.[25] The CMGF Center coordinates closely with the 14 provinces and local governments regarding IMT-GT strategies programs and projects and makes the proposals to the national secretariat and senior officials.

Coordination for Spatial Planning

In the IMT-GT Vision 2036, the spatial approach to regional development has been mentioned as one of the guiding principles. Since the present system of project planning emanates from the sectors, NESDC ensures that the project is aligned with the plans for the development of the SEC.

For all connectivity projects, the motorways–rails map is used as a guide for future development of infrastructure for the whole country.[26] For example, the motorways–rails map has specified that a new land bridge will be needed to link across Southern Thailand at Chumphon–Ranong and at Surat Thani–Phuket. Before this, only the regional plans were utilized. The Ministry of Interior has divided the southern region into three clusters: (i) the Andaman provinces from Ranong to Satun; (ii) Gulf of Thailand cluster from Chumphon to Songkhla; and (iii) the three southernmost provinces of Pattani, Yala, and Narathiwat. Each cluster is headed by the most senior governor, while the cluster committees are chaired by the other governors.

Coordination between Government and Private Sector

The involvement of the private sector in economic corridor development is done through the cluster committees. The head or chair of business organizations are invited to attend the cluster meetings, which are convened frequently. Line ministries follow the clustering system of the Ministry of Interior since their provincial units are attached to the office of the provincial governors.

---

[25]   SBPAC shall have powers and duties in the southern border provinces to prepare action plans, which shall be implemented in the southern border provinces in accordance with the southern border provinces development strategies, https://www.krisdika.go.th/data// document/ext810/810243_0001.pdf.

[26]   The motorways–rails map is the transportation development masterplan of the development of transportation networks linking production bases, agriculture, industry to consumers and international markets that help reduce logistics costs. The development will involve the development of motorways, new railways, double track railways, and high-speed train, and connecting points to all transportation models; roads, rails, and ports in three north–south and six east–west corridors of Thailand. https://motapplication. mot.go.th/mot-api/03-brain/upload/Magazine//814747_%E0%B8%A3%E0%B8%B2%E0%B8%8A%E0%B8%A3%E0%B8%96- %E0%B9%80%E0%B8%A1%E0%B8%A9.pdf.

The JBC is the official voice of the private sector in the IMT-GT. The JBC is invited to participate in meetings of working groups, senior officials, ministers, and national secretariats to give their views and perspectives on various initiatives. They can also propose and participate in IMT-GT projects.

The JBC has a chapter in each of the three countries. JBC-Thailand is composed of the Thailand Chamber of Commerce, Federation of Thai Industries, Bankers Association of Thailand, and representatives from the 14 southern provinces. However, the relationship between the central unit and the provincial units still needs to be improved and strengthened in terms of joint initiatives and coming up with good project proposals. The JBC also needs to be more proactive in providing strategic inputs to the development of economic corridors, especially in identifying business and value chain opportunities.

Coordination for Economic Corridor Development

The implementations of economic corridor development is a complex process involving various stakeholders in many sectors at different coordination levels. To implement projects and plans effectively, stakeholders and agencies must work closely at all coordination levels.

The CMGF must promote a better understanding of the concept of economic corridors at the provincial levels. Provinces and states in the three countries belonging to an economic corridor can be organized into a cluster or committee at the subregional level to discuss programs, projects, and strategies.

At the national level, economic corridor development committees can also be organized. The committee can be composed of representatives from the provincial government, the private sector (including JBC), the CMGF secretariat, and SBPAC. The SBPAC has the authority and responsibility for the development in Songkhla, Pattani, Yala, Narathiwat, and Satun, and can provide strategic guidance.[27] The economic corridor development committees can also focus on stimulating and implementing projects and plans in the corridors, such as promotion of tourism, improvements in trade facilitation at the border or gateway ports, and promotion of business opportunity for subregional supply chains.

CMGF Thailand works closely with the NESDC, the JBC, and working groups to formulate and implement corridor strategies, programs, and projects. The CMGF secretariats of Indonesia, Malaysia, and Thailand should work more closely together to coordinate their strategies, programs, and projects to enhance economic corridor development.

At the subregional level, an occasional forum could be established where subnational bodies (e.g., The East Coast Economic Region Development Council [ECERDC], Northern Corridor Implementation Authority [NCIA], Southern Thailand Economic Development body, and Sumatera development body) can meet and discuss strategic issues on economic corridor development.

---

27   Government of Thailand. 2010. Southern Border Provinces Administration Act. https://www.krisdika.go.th/data//document/ext810/810243_0001.pdf. Section 3. pp. 1.

Recommendations

- The IMT-GT minister should also be the minister in charge of economic affairs or for the NESDC. It should be the DPM.

- An occasional forum could be established where subnational bodies (e.g., ECERDC, NCIA, Southern Thailand Economic Development body, Sumatera development body) can come together to discuss strategic issues on economic corridor development including the implications of post-pandemic recovery plans and scenarios.

- The CMGF could be made more effective by encouraging the national CMGF units to interact more closely and frequently in between the annual meetings of the CMGF. The initial step in this direction is to strengthen the national CMGF units. In the case of Thailand, the role of CMGF Center taken by the Prince of Songkhla University has been efficient and is well-funded by the Ministry of Interior through an annual budget. The CMGF Center (Thailand) should be encouraged to work more closely with its counterparts in Indonesia and Malaysia.

- The JBC needs to be more proactive in economic corridor development initiatives. It needs to reach out to all levels of stakeholders—the micro, small, and medium-sized enterprises, young entrepreneurs, and new start-ups.

- The Centre for IMT-GT Subregional Cooperation would need to have a sharper focus on economic corridor development for its midterm review of the implementation blueprint for 2017–2021 and for the new implementation blueprint for 2022–2026.

CHAPTER

8

SUMMARY OF FINDINGS
AND RECOMMENDATIONS

The assessment of the Thailand component of the economic corridors focuses on (i) the status and physical condition of transport infrastructure, (ii) and cross-border connectivity and cross-border nodes, (iii) trade and tourism, and (iv) economic potential including value chain opportunities.

Overall, the transport infrastructure in EC1, EC2, EC5, and EC6 are in good condition, especially for roads. However, there are missing links in the corridors especially, along the border between Thailand and Malaysia. At present, there are no cross-border trains between Malaysia and Thailand in EC1, rail connectivity along EC2 in Thailand is limited, no maritime trade has developed between ports in EC5, and air linkages between nodes in the corridors are generally undeveloped. To enhance corridor connectivity, the following are recommended:

Economic Corridor 1: Multimodal transportation will need to be further developed. EC1 contributes the highest overland trade in the country. The transport system is dominated by land, and to a lesser extent by rail, which are used to transport agricultural produce from plantations to factories. Goods are then transported through the Thailand–Malaysia borders and further to the ports along the Strait of Malacca to export destinations. An important transport system is the land route used to transport goods between the southern region and the central plains of Thailand. Songkhla Port serves as the maritime gateway port connecting the IMT-GT subregion to the GMS in Laem Chabang, Chonburi Province. Songkhla Port also connects to Penang Port passing through the Thailand–Malaysian borders. Utilizing Thong Song CDC in Nakhon Si Thammarat by connecting with Kantang Port by rail, to Port Klang in Malaysia is a vital alternative.

Songkhla Port II needs to be developed to connect to Penang Port under the land bridge concept, which would reduce the time and cost of transporting goods between the two ocean coasts.

Upgrading of cross-border facilities can reduce the time and costs to trade. Sadao BCP has the highest land trade in Thailand but is congested due to the high volume of trade and tourists. Sadao (Songkhla) and Bukit Kayu Hitam (Kedah) Customs houses have completed new Customs facilities and can now operate more efficiently.

Padang Besa (Songkhla) and Padang Besar (Perlis) BCP will complement the Sadao–Bukit Kayu Hitam area. Padang Besar BCP is the gateway for transporting goods from Thailand to Malaysia via road and rail. The goods are then transported to Penang Port to be shipped to export markets. Padang Besa BCP has the potential to increase the volume of rail transportation due to transshipment and transit of goods at the border although there is no ICD to facilitate rail logistics in Padang Besa, Thailand.

Ban Prakop is a new border crossing with modern CIQ and ICQS facilities and good road facilities on both sides of the border. It has great potential to promote new development in the area and offers a great alternative as an import–export channel due to less traffic.

Strengthening the domestic value chain can create a great opportunity for SMEs to participate in subregional and global border value chains. EC1 is the area concentrated on agriculture and agro-based industries for palm oil, rubber, seafood, and livestock. Enhancing the production of these commodities can open opportunities for SMEs to link with subregional and global supply chains or market.

Economic Corridor 2: Ports connectivity will need to be further developed. The main agricultural products in EC2 are palm oil, rubber, and fruits. Farmers' produce are sent to processing factories in Chumphon, Surat Thani, and Songkhla. Kantang Port is the only port that connects with the southern railway system at Thong Song CDC in Nakhon Si Thammarat. It transports bulk goods, and containerized goods.

Therefore, Kantang Port has a high potential to become major gateway for exporting cargoes to Port Klang in Malaysia and other ports in Indonesia. Moreover, this can stimulate multimodal transport through ports in Satun to Aceh and Belawan Ro-Ro ferry service is planned to be piloted between Belawan–Penang–Satun.

Tourism can make a major economic contribution to Economic Corridor 2. Phuket and Krabi are well-known international tourism nodes. Connecting tourism along the coasts of the Andaman Sea from Phuket, Krabi, Trang, and Satun will integrate the tourism route in the EC2 onward to Malaysia and Indonesia.

Economic Corridor 5 is in a strategic position to become a maritime gateway connecting to BIMSTEC and the rest of IMT-GT and a tourism hub for Thailand. Ranong Port is underutilized as no cargo is being transported from there to any port in IMT-GT. Ranong Port supports an oil rig in the Andaman Sea. The Port Authority of Thailand would need to expedite action on the memorandum of understanding with Navayuga Container Terminal and Krishna Patnam Port, India—which is one of the ports of BIMSTEC member countries—to facilitate trade and transportation between the two subregions.

The promotion of cruise lines and yacht tourism can attract more tourists to Economic Corridor 5. Phuket is a well-known tourism destination in this region. However, Phuket Deep Sea Port is designed as a pier for handling goods. In recent years, more cruises have visited Phuket Port, and the number is increasing every year. Phuket Port has the potential to accommodate and service large cruise ships and eventually become a homeport. Yacht tourism in Phuket has also been increasing every year. There is high potential for Krabi and Phuket to become a yacht tourism and maintenance hub for the IMT-GT subregion.

Economic Corridor 6: The development should focus not only cross-border trade but also cross-border value chains. EC6's main economic activities include agriculture, agro-industry, and trade. The provinces in the EC6 are facing security issues that limit investment. Therefore, agriculture products are usually transported and processed in nearby provincial factories or exported directly along the Thailand–Malaysia borders (Tak Bai, Buketa, Su-ngai Kolok, and Betong). Agriculture, and agro-based Industry include rubber, fruit, seafood, and livestock. To promote the EC6 development effectively, development approach should promote and strengthen domestic value chain especially for SMEs, then connect to cross-border value chain with Malaysia, especially halal food and products.

Infrastructure linkages will stimulate trade, investment, and tourism between Thailand, Malaysia, and Indonesia. The EC6 has overland routes from Pattani to Penang Port and further to Port Klang. The EC6 also connects maritime gateways at Kuantan Port (Pahang). Kuantan Port is the designated port for the PRC–Malaysia BRI and plays a strategic role in expanding trade with PRC and Europe. This connectivity will promote the three southernmost provinces of Pattani, Yala, and Narathiwat (EC6) for trading to the wider markets (Map 20). Some missing links must be addressed to fully realize the potential of EC6.

(i)   Constructing (a) the second bridge across Kolok River at Su-ngai Kolok–Rantau Panjang; (b) the bridge over Kolok River at Tak Bai–Pengkalan Kubur; and (iii) upgrading the Thailand–Malaysia Friendship bridge across Kolok River at Buketa–Bukit Bunga to facilitate the transport of rubber and other cargoes to Kelantan, Kuantan, and Penang Ports in Malaysia;

(ii)   Connecting the railway route from Su-ngai Kolok Railway Station to Pasir Mas Railway Station in Kelantan Malaysia covering 20 km (2 km in Thailand and 18 km in Malaysia) to create an alternative rubber product transport route via Kuantan Port to the PRC (Kuantan Port has been designated as the BRI Port connecting to the PRC);

(iii)   Stimulating the establishment of Narathiwat SEZ to promote and attract investors in processed rubber, rubber wood, and halal food industries that can generate employment and incomes in EC6.

Map 20: Six Indonesia–Malaysia–Thailand Growth Triangle Economic Corridors

INDONESIA–MALAYSIA–THAILAND GROWTH TRIANGLE

Southwestern Thailand–Northern Sumatera–Northwestern Malaysia Economic Corridor (Reconfigured EC5)

Southern Thailand–Northern Malaysia–North Sumatera Economic Corridor (Reconfigured EC1)

Andaman Sea–Strait of Malacca Economic Corridor (Reconfigured EC2)

Central Sumatera–Southern Malaysia Economic Corridor (Reconfigured EC4)

Southeastern Thailand–Eastern Malaysia–Southern Sumatera Economic Corridor (EC6)

Trans-Sumatera Economic Corridor (Reconfigured EC3)

Economic Corridor 1 Reconfiguration
Economic Corridor 2 Reconfiguration
Economic Corridor 3 Reconfiguration
Economic Corridor 4 Reconfiguration
Economic Corridor 5 Reconfiguration
Proposed Economic Corridor 6

0   50 100 150 200 250
Kilometers

THAILAND
PENINSULAR MALAYSIA
SINGAPORE
INDONESIA

Andaman Sea
Strait of Malacca
Java Sea
INDIAN OCEAN

National Capital
Provincial/State Capital
City/Town
Airport
National Road
Other Road
Provincial Boundary
International Boundary
EC = economic corridor
Boundaries are not necessarily authoritative.

This map was produced by the cartography unit of the Asian Development Bank. The boundaries, colors, denominations, and any other information shown on this map do not imply, on the part of the Asian Development Bank, any judgment on the legal status of any territory, or any endorsement or acceptance of such boundaries, colors, denominations, or information.

Source: Asian Development Bank.

APPENDIXES

Appendix 1

Projects Under the Indonesia–Malaysia–Thailand Growth Triangle Action Plan

The Extended Songkhla–Penang-Medan Economic Corridor (EC1) route consists of five projects: (i) Pier Development Project, (ii) construction of expressway, (iii) construction of double-track railway, (iv) establishment of SEZ, and (v) Rubber City (Table A1.1).

Table A1.1: Projects under the Extended Songkhla–Penang–Medan Economic Corridor (Economic Corridor 1) Route

Items	Projects	Details	Budget (B million)	Years in operation
Surat Thani				
1	Development of Standard Pier for Tourism	Cruise tourism is growing and the market is expanding. Visitors are quality tourists with quite high expenses per person per day. Tourism in the southern coasts on the Gulf of Thailand still lacks a main pier to accommodate large cruise ships. The development of marine basic infrastructure and standard port will increase tourism potential. A pier for large cruise ships to accommodate marine tourism in Koh Samui area will stimulate growth in trade, industry, and investment in the southern region.		2018–2021
Songkhla				
2	Construction of Expressway Hat Yai–Sadao	Project to construct expressway between Hat Yai–Malaysian border covering 63.5 kilometers (km). Currently the project passed an environmental impact assessment and is in the process of budget proposal for the study of detailed design and public–private partnership funding model in 2021.		2020
3	Construction of Double-Track Railway Surat Thani–Hat Yai–Padang Besar	Project to construct a double-track railway Surat Thani-Hat Yai–Padang Besar covering of 366 km. The area under the study covers the side distance of 500 meters from the center of the route passing four provinces: Surat Thani, Nakhon Si Thammarat, Phatthalung, and Songkhla with 58 stations between Surat Thani and Hat Yai Junction and seven stations between Hat Yai Junction and Songkhla. It is currently seeking budget from the government.		2024–2028

continued on next page

Table A1.1 continued

Items	Projects	Details	Budget (B million)	Years in operation
4	Establishment of Special Economic Zone	The establishment of Songkhla Special Economic Zone in 1,196 rai[a] at Samnak Kham subdistrict, Sadao District is in the process of adjusting the area appropriate to industrial estate, distribution center, and one-stop service. Investors have already invested in three projects valued B893 million in pure coconut oil extraction, rubber glove production, and latex production. At present, Songkhla has set up a one-stop service for investment at Sadao District.	900 (Phase 1)	2018–2022
5	Rubber City	Rubber City is in the Southern Region Industrial Estate. The objective is to serve as a rubber market that can produce new products, higher value-added, more efficiency and sustainability. It is in the process of constructing a factory and adjusting the area, as well as seeking interested investors. Entrepreneurs have built two plants in the area and small and medium-sized enterprises have rented seven standard factory buildings.	1,677.96	2018–2022

[a] Rai is a Thai unit of area equivalent to 1,600 square meters.
Sources: Surat Thani Provincial Development Plan 2020 and Songkhla Provincial Development Plan 2020.

The Strait of Malacca Economic Corridor (EC2) Route consists of three projects: (i) Customs checkpoint development, (ii) construction of a bridge connecting two countries, and (iii) expansion of port services (Table A1.2).

Table A1.2: Projects under the Strait of Malacca Economic Corridor (Economic Corridor 2) Route

Items	Projects	Details	Budget (B million)	Years of operation
Satun				
1	Development of Customs Checkpoint Wang Prachan–Wang Kelian	The project will establish a one-stop Customs checkpoint. The design of the structure and facilities of transport is done and the project is in the process of conducting an environmental impact assessment. The southern border provinces have provided B816,5000 to improve the checkpoint building of Wang Prachan with the investment budget of B7,765,000. A workshop to publicize the trade and tourism route between Thailand–Malaysia with the operating budget of B400,000 has been organized.		2020
2	Construction of New Bridge connecting Satun and Perlis	The project will construct a 14-km bridge connecting Satun and Perlis along the coasts of Tam Malang, Mueang Satun District, to Koh Puyu, Puyu subdistrict, and then to Perlis in Malaysia. The bridge will help solve transport problems, accelerate the province's economic growth, and generate more income in the area, leading to the region's stable, prosperous, and sustainable economic system.		2020
Trang				
3	Project to expand services provided to Ban Na Kluea Pier	The Ban Na Kluea Pier is at Na Kluea Subdistrict, Kantang District, in the area of 100 rai.[a] It can accommodate simultaneously two bulk cargo ships of 4,000 tons gross. It responds to the needs of transporting goods around the coasts in the Andaman Sea and increases potential to accommodate more goods in the port in Trang. It also expands prosperity to the outer areas, generating employment and distributing income. It is currently in the process of establishing the Customs office building providing one-stop service.	406	2020

km = kilometer.
[a] Rai is a Thai unit of area equivalent to 1,600 square meters.
Sources: Satun Provincial Development Plan 2020 and Trang Provincial Development Plan 2020.

The projects under the Ranong–Phuket–Aceh Economic Corridor (EC5) route consists of four projects to improve and construct the basic infrastructure in transport and logistics to facilitate loading and unloading of goods and passengers. The projects include the improvement of the port and airport, and development of a public transport system (Table A1.3).

Table A1.3: Projects under the Ranong–Phuket–Aceh Economic Corridor (Economic Corridor 5) Route

Items	Projects	Details	Budget (B million)	Years of Operation
Ranong				
1	Improvement of Ranong Port	Improvement of Ranong Port consists of maintenance and repair of the basic infrastructure in the port and construction of facilities for shipment (such as repair of the structure of piers 1 and 2, construction of pier 3 with 180 meters long and 30 meters wide, construction of container yard for piers 1–3, installation of labor-saving devices, dredging in front of the pier area for 500 meters long, and formulation of marketing promotion plan).	5,471	2019–2022
2	Improvement of Ranong Airport	This project will improve facilities, construction, and installation of airport safety equipment (such as improvement of high- and low-voltage electrical system in passenger terminal, construction of fences surrounding the aviation area, installation of security system, and installation of weapon and explosive detectors).	158.62	2019–2020
Phuket				
3	Development of Phuket Deep Sea Port	The project will expand the pier and construct mooring, specifically: expansion of the pier from 360 meters to 420 meters to facilitate transport and loading and unloading of goods, construction of one-floor passenger terminal, construction of a bridge and three pontoons in front of the pier, and construction of mooring in the sea and on land.	132	2019–2020
4	Construction of Light Rail	The project will construct Phuket's mass transit system project, between Phuket International Airport–Chalong Intersection with 21 stations (about 42 kilometers).	34,827.28	2019–2024

Sources: Ranong Provincial Development Plan 2020 and Phuket Provincial Development Plan 2020.

The Southeastern Thailand–Eastern Malaysia–Southern Sumatera Economic Corridor (EC6) route includes 15 projects. Most projects are under the "Triangle of Stability, Prosperity, and Sustainability" model. The areas of the model city include Su-ngai Kolok District, Narathiwat (to develop the center of cross-border trade), Nong Chik District, Pattani (to develop the model city of agro-processing industry), and Betong District, Yala (to develop the model city of sustainable self-reliance) (Table A1.4).

Table A1.4: Projects under the Southeastern Thailand–Eastern Malaysia–Southern Sumatera Economic Corridor (Economic Corridor 6) Route

Items	Projects	Details	Budget (B million)	Years in operation
Narathiwat				
1	Narathiwat Special Economic Zone Development Project	The Narathiwat Special Economic Zone Development Project is at Lahan Subdistrict, Yi-ngo District, and Kok Kian Subdistrict, Mueang District, Narathiwat, with the total area of 1,683 rai.[a] The objective is to serve as the area to process products and encourage employment of local residents with seven targeted industrial groups such as labor-intensive industries (textile and garment), furniture industry, wood-processed furniture, halal industry, upstream and midstream rubber processing industries, industries with customers' base in Malaysia, or relying on raw materials from Malaysia, or other service industries not affecting the environment.	2,593.70	2020
		Three agencies are responsible for the management of the area. The Industrial Estate Authority of Thailand manages the area of 600 rai. The remaining area of 1,083 rai will be managed by the Treasury Department together with Narathiwat Province. The area will be allocated to small and medium-sized enterprises in the three southern border provinces (Pattani, Yala, Narathiwat) for 300 rai.		
		Around 31 entrepreneurs are interested in investing in the development area with the total area of 1,160 rai, divided by business categories. There are six entrepreneurs in rubber business with the total area of 120 rai, nine entrepreneurs in halal business (food and non-food) with the total area of 210 rai, four entrepreneurs in alternative energy business with the total area of 330 rai, two entrepreneurs in plastic business with the total area of 30 rai, eight entrepreneurs in other business with the total area of 270 rai, and two entrepreneurs with no specified business with the total area of 200 rai.		
		The entrepreneurs who will invest in Narathiwat Special Economic Zone will receive twice the incentives compared to other zones in the country. They will receive incentives according to the announcement of the temporary special economic zone of Narathiwat and incentives according to the announcement of special economic zone covering incentives on tax, finance, and incentives according to the announcement of Board of Investments, with 231 businesses with investment promotion.		

continued on next page

Table A1.4 continued

Items	Projects	Details	Budget (B million)	Years in operation
2	Buketa Customs Checkpoint Expansion Project	Buketa Customs Checkpoint Expansion Project covers the Thai–Malaysian Bridge at Lochut Subdistrict, Waeng District, Narathiwat to the current Buketa Customs Checkpoint. It covers the communities that border Kolok River on both the Thai and Malaysian sides (community of Bukit Bunga, Kelantan). The future economic growth forecasts the increase in the area's trade, transit, and tourism on a continuous basis. There will be an increase of population in Jeli, which is 11 kilometers from Bukit Bunga Checkpoint and home of Universiti Malaysia Kelantan and Politeknik Jeli (under construction). It is expected to have about 4,000 students upon completion. Waeng District is also home to Hala-Bala Wildlife Sanctuary. The border community tends to become more congested. The possibility of transporting processed wood between Thailand–Malaysia–Singapore will make the logistics center clearer to accommodate the transport through Buketa Customs Checkpoint.	430.24	
3	Bridge over Kolok River at Tak Bai District with Customs Checkpoint Building	The new bridge across Kolok River at Tak Bai District, Narathiwat, and Pengkalan Kubor, Kelantan will directly connect Mueang District, Narathiwat; and Kota Bharu, the state capital of Kelantan, without having to travel by ferry or without having to make a detour via Su-ngai Kolok District (reducing the distance by 40 kilometers). It will stimulate economic development between lower southern region and Kelantan and Terengganu and other areas in the East Coast Economic Region of Malaysia. The bridge will promote and support the special economic zones at the borders between Narathiwat and Pasir Mas Halal Park in Kelantan. The Department of Highways has submitted the detailed design to Malaysia for review.	21.0	2020
4	Narathiwat Airport Development Project	The passenger terminal at Narathiwat Airport has been in disrepair due to long usage. The number of passengers has also increased, leading to congestion, especially during the Hajj and the Umrah. Moreover, the increased flights damage the runway. The project will lengthen the runway, repair of the runway surface, and improve the passenger terminal to sufficiently accommodate passengers and the economic growth in the area and the special economic zone in the future. The construction of the new passenger terminal will be in accordance with the safety standards of an airport. It consists of the installation of two weapon and explosive detectors type Dual View X-ray with the size of 100 cm x 100 cm and two more detectors with the size of 60 cm x 40 cm.	836.88	2020–2022

continued on next page

Table A1.4 continued

Items	Projects	Details	Budget (B million)	Years in operation
5	Railway Route Improvement Project between Su-ngai Kolok–Rantau Panjang–Tumpat	The project to improve railway route from Su-ngai Kolok Railway Station to Pasir Mas Railway Station, Kelantan, in Malaysia covers 20 kilometers (the distance of 2 kilometers in Thailand and 18 kilometers in Malaysia), which has stopped service for 20 years. If the railway route is improved, it will connect Tumpat Station, Kelantan to Johor, and then to Singapore. It will increase convenience and connect the networks of traveling and transporting goods. The State Railway of Thailand has finished the improvement of the railway route from Hat Yai Station to Rantau Panjang Station. It improved 100 pounds of the basic structure of the rail and monoblock concrete railroad tie. It can transport goods via containers. But transportation is still not possible, pending the improvement of the basic structure of the rail in Malaysia.		2020
6	Construction of the Second Bridge over Kolok River at Su-ngai Kolok–Rantau Panjang	This is a joint project between Thailand and Malaysia. Malaysia has finished the design, which will be sent to Thailand for review.	180.00	
7	Duty Free City Project	Although Narathiwat is a border city, there are still no duty free shops or zones. It is therefore necessary to set up a duty free zone to attract both domestic and international tourists to promote trade, purchases, and sales of goods, (wholesale and retail). At present, Narathiwat has sent invitation letters to those interested to submit the rate of rents of land and buildings, as well as business plan in establishing a duty free shop at OTOP Center, Su-ngai Kolok District.	5.17	2020
8	Improvement and Upgrading of Su-ngai Kolok Railway Station and Establishment of Inventory Station Project	The project will improve the area around Su-ngai Kolok Railway Station, construction of container yard and warehouse. A feasibility study and design of the details covering 78 rai in Su-ngai Kolok Subdistrict has been done.	707.22	

continued on next page

Table A1.4 continued

Items	Projects	Details	Budget (B million)	Years in operation
Pattani				
9	Construction Project of Southern Border Animal Market to Accommodate Halal Industry	The project will promote and support the development of the province into a center of fresh food, frozen food, and processed food for domestic, international, and digital trade for stable growth, focusing on agro-industry, fishery, and livestock.		2020
10	City of Health Food Processing and Halal Food	The project will develop a city of health food processing and halal food plants, focusing on quality, export standards, and environmental-friendly characteristics.		2020
11	City of Wholesale, Retail, and Service of Southern Border Provinces	The project will connect the trade of southern border provinces with southern countries in Association of Southeast Asian Nations, and as a modern city to accommodate digital society and connecting point of the southern border provinces.		
Yala				
12	Raw Materials for Halal Food	The project will focus on the development of livestock in the area such as breeding of local chicken, breeding of Betong chicken, breeding of duck for meat, breeding of goat for milk, breeding of beef cattle, and animal feed production.		2020
13	Integrated Agro-Processing Plant	The project will increase efficiency in processing agricultural produces, increase value of agricultural produces, and serve as knowledge center, research, and development, by focusing on employment, income generation of farmers, community enterprises, and local residents. The targeted areas in the three districts include Than To District, Betong District, and Banang Sata District.		2020

ᵃ Rai is a Thai unit of area equivalent to 1,600 square meters.
Source: Narathiwat Provincial Development Plan 2020, Pattani Provincial Development Plan 2020, and Yala Provincial Development Plan 2020.

Appendix 2

Ministries and Agencies Involved during the Country Consultations

A. Ministries and Agencies That Met during the Fieldwork Conducted by the Study Team on 11–15 November 2019

- National Secretariat, National Economic and Social Development Council
- Ministry of Transport
- Sadao Custom
- Ban Prakop Custom
- Betong Custom
- Narathiwat Governor
- Buketa Custom
- Su-ngai Kolok Custom
- Narathiwat Chamber of Commerce
- Narathiwat Federation of Thai Industry
- Pattani Chamber of Commerce
- Pattani Federation of Thai Industry
- Yala Custom
- Yala Provincial Office
- Yala Chamber of Commerce
- Yala Federation of Thai Industry
- Southern Border Provinces Administration Centre

B. Departments and Agencies That Participated during Various Consultation Meetings by the National Consultant with the National Secretariat

- Department of Land Transport
- Department of Highways
- Marine Department
- Industrial Estate Authority of Thailand
- The Civil Aviation Authority of Thailand
- Department of Foreign Trade
- Port Authority of Thailand

www.ingramcontent.com/pod-product-compliance
Lightning Source LLC
Chambersburg PA
CBHW061220270326
41926CB00032B/4793